DEFENDING
EVERYBODY

DEFENDING EVERYBODY

A HISTORY OF THE AMERICAN CIVIL LIBERTIES UNION

Diane Garey

New York

Publisher's Cataloging-in-Publication Data
Garey, Diane
    Defending everybody : a history of the American Civil Liberties Union / Diane Garey. — 1st ed.
        p. cm.
    Includes bibliographical references.
    ISBN: 1-57500-066-0
    1. American Civil Liberties Union—History. 2. Civil rights—History—United States. I. Title.
    JC599.U5G37 1998   323'.06'073
                                          QBI98-935

The publisher has made every effort to secure permission to reproduce copyrighted material and would like to apologize should there have been any errors or omissions.

TV Books, L.L.C.
Publishers serving the television industry.
1619 Broadway, Ninth Floor
New York, NY 10019
www.tvbooks.com

For Larry and Katie

Contents

Acknowledgments

Defending Everybody is a selective history, one that presents a few of the cases that exemplify the ACLU's growth from gadfly to Goliath. In some instances—as, for example, the Scopes case—I chose the more famous. In others—such as the Levy court-martial and the Chicago Housing battle—I chose to write about cases that quite simply interested me. This book has evolved in tandem with the PBS documentary film "The ACLU: A History," co-produced with KCTS, Public Television in Seattle. Lawrence R. Hott is the producer and director of this film: my first thanks go to him.

I also thank the many people who agreed to be interviewed for the film and book in the fall and winter of 1996: Carl Baldwin, Julian Bond, Dave Barry, The Rev. George Clements, Roger Connor, Chester Darling, William Donohue, Norman Dorsen, Stanley Fish, Ira Glasser, David Goldberger, Nat Hentoff, Molly Ivins, Harvey Grossman, John Leo, Howard Levy, Anthony Lewis, Ernest Matthews, Mary McAuliffe, Jay Miller, Charles Morgan Jr., Burt Neuborne, Eleanor Holmes Norton, Oliver North, Roger Pilon, Mark Pratt, Artensa Randolph, Alan Reitman, Ramona Ripston, Loren Siegel, Norman Siegel, Nadine Strossen, and Ethyl Washington.

I am particularly grateful to Loren Siegel at the national office of the ACLU, and to the national and affiliate staff, and I would like to thank those who worked on the film: Writer Ken Chowder; Narrator Joe Mantegna; Cinematographer Allen Moore; Composer Richard Einhorn; Assistant Editor Susan Orlosky; Associate Producer Joan E. Kane; Consultants Joshua

Cohen, Robert Cottrell, Owen Fiss, David Garrow, Richard Immerman, Judy Kutulas, Mary McAuliffe, Ellen Schrecker, Bert Neuborne, and Samuel Walker; Archival Research Frank Ortega and Lisa Wright Dupuy; John G. Avildsen for the Roger Baldwin interview from the film *Traveling Hopefully* and Sheila Shamovitz for film footage from *Skokie: Rights or Wrong?*; and archival materials from the American Civil Liberties Union, Seeley G. Mudd Library–Princeton University, John E. Allen, Library of Congress, National Archives, Taminent Institute Library–New York University, and Sophia Smith Collection–Smith College.

My thanks also to the film's funders—the Floyd and Delores Jones Foundation, the Open Society Institute, the Playboy Foundation, the Illinois Humanities Council, and the Massachusetts Foundation for the Humanities—and, of course, to Peter Kaufman and TV Books for believing in this project from the outset.

"The ACLU files more lawsuits than the Justice Department. They're the biggest law firm in America. They're an enormously powerful institution."
　　　　　—Roger Conner, Center for the Community Interest

"They live, I think, in a dreamland of abstraction where speech just exists in this wonderful world as if the entire world were a philosophy seminar and nothing of consequence ever came of it."
　　　　　—Stanley Fish, Professor of English
　　　　　and Law, Duke University

"I'm afraid that the ACLU does not have the gift of making itself popular. Supporting the Bill of Rights, in fact, generally makes you about as popular as a whore trying to get into the S.M.U. Theology School."
　　　　　—Molly Ivins, author and syndicated columnist

Introduction

On November 11, 1918, the Great War ended. Americans woke up to a cacophony of fire alarms, church bells, and factory whistles. In every city in the country people paraded through the streets, dancing, singing, waving flags. But in Newark, New Jersey, one man was not dancing or singing, and he was not waving an American flag. That Armistice Day, Roger Baldwin, thirty-four years old, entered federal prison. He spent nine months there, quietly gardening, thinking . . . and planning an organization that would cause controversy—and create enemies—for the rest of the twentieth century.

On paper, the organization he founded seemed harmless: the American Civil Liberties Union was created to support the individual liberties guaranteed by the Bill of Rights. But the organization supported the rights of the individual against the majority and the government. For eighty years, this has ignited rage in liberals and conservatives alike. The ACLU has been accused of all manner of outrageous behavior. They've been called "socially illiterate" and "anti-religious." A spokesman for the National Lawyers Guild once accused them of a "poisonous even-handedness" in their choice of clients. William Donohue, of the Catholic League for Religious and Civil Rights, says that the ACLU is "intoxicated with the idea of individual rights to such an extent that it actually works, however unwittingly, to destroy the moral foundation of our society." Writer and law professor Stanley Fish characterized the ACLU this way: "When I describe the ACLU to anyone I say 'think of an organization that goes out and finds things it hates, and then grows them. Wouldn't you find that a little peculiar?'"

In fact, the ACLU is peculiar. Most civil liberties groups are defense organizations, set up to protect a particular group (Jews, Communists, African-Americans, prisoners) while staying largely indifferent to everyone else. The ACLU, it has been said, "loves no one, but helps anyone whose rights have been violated." The business of the ACLU, then, is the defense of everybody. It has defended the rights of presidents, labor organizers, school children, and despicable criminals. It has defended flamboyant personalities like Muhammad Ali and Larry Flynt, liberals like Julian Bond, and ultraconservatives like Oliver North. It has even defended the right to free speech of those who don't believe in free speech—Ku Klux Klansmen, Communists, and Nazis—sometimes cheerfully, sometimes reluctantly. "It makes my skin crawl to think of some of the guys that we had to represent over the years," said Burt Neuborne, former legal director of the Union. "It's like taking out the garbage. [But] somebody's got to take the garbage out."

"We're reasonable people, despite some of the activities in which we are engaged," ACLU founder Roger Baldwin insisted. "We've become a rather respectable, established institution." Baldwin could claim a measure of respectability for his controversial group: since its founding in 1920 some of the most admired legal minds in the country have worked on ACLU cases. Clarence Darrow, Felix Frankfurter, Osmond Fraenkel, and Eleanor Holmes Norton all have, at one time or another, served as counsel to clients that the ACLU has chosen to defend. But the notoriety of the client list has had quite an effect on the reputation of the ACLU; it is perceived not as a legal organization representing the rights of extremists, but rather as extremist itself, in cahoots with racists and radicals.

The ACLU's public stance on its cases has contributed to its unpopularity. "What makes me the most frustrated about the ACLU," said Roger Connor of the Center for the Community Interest, "is their self-righteous arrogance. They think the Constitution is the Bible, and they think they're the Pope." It's an arrogance that originated with Baldwin, who loved to lecture anyone who would listen about the purist nature of the ACLU's mission. "It's the Bill of Rights we're defending," he pronounced, time and time again.

Not surprisingly, this high moral tone infuriated others, time and time again. Patriotic Americans were furious when the ACLU stood up for the free speech rights of pacifists after World War I. More recently, Jewish concentration camp survivors were enraged when the ACLU supported the rights of Nazis to sport swastikas in a 1977 demonstration in Skokie, Illinois (home to a number of Holocaust survivors). Both these cases were of the kind closest to Roger Baldwin's heart: free speech, clearly protected by the First Amendment, has been supported by the ACLU since its founding. But the ACLU has taken on cases that have moved beyond Baldwin's original passion for the First Amendment. Chicago public housing residents were angered in 1993 when the ACLU argued that safety measures introduced by the Housing Authority violated the Fourth Amendment rights of the same residents. "We didn't want the ACLU here," said Artensa Randolph, a community leader and public housing resident who supported the measures. "Certainly people in public housing were not saying that they want to let people trample over their Fourth Amendment rights," said Father George Clements, a Chicago-based priest and community activist. "All we are saying to the ACLU is that if you're living in dangerous circumstances, and if you get killed, what good is the Fourth Amendment?" In a world where personal safety is more prized than personal freedom, the ACLU will indeed find itself unwelcome.

"We live in an era that takes the Bill of Rights for granted," said Burt Neuborne. "We take free speech for granted, we take due process for granted. We tend to forget that these rights are only about sixty years old. They are only about as old as the ACLU." Even the most vehement critics agree that, for better or worse, the ACLU's tinkering with the Bill of Rights has molded our national idea of liberty—and shaped what we call the American way of life.

Chapter 1

Making Laws for the Human Mind:
The Bill of Rights Before 1917

*The Bill of Rights is an extraordinary document. If anything
has ever been close to perfect, the First Amendment is it. And,
of course, Madison wrote it up in so few words. As a writer,
I can only sit here in envy.*

—Molly Ivins

James Madison was thirty-five years old, a bachelor, and a member of the Virginia State Assembly when he fought his first great battle for religious freedom in the United States. The year was 1786, and the fiery patriot Patrick Henry was promoting state support for teachers of the Christian religion in Virginia. Madison, continuing a separation of church and state campaign that Thomas Jefferson had begun, went head-to-head with Henry—and won. Under his leadership, the Assembly approved Virginia's Statute of Religious Freedom. This statute, wrote Madison, would "extinguish forever the ambitious hope of making laws for the human mind."

It was in this spirit that, three years later, as a member of the U.S. House of Representatives, Madison wrote the set of Amendments to the U.S. Constitution that would become the

Bill of Rights. But here Madison was motivated as much by politics as by his belief in freedom. The Constitution was a young document under siege—it had been ratified by the states in 1788, but strongly criticized for putting too much power in the hands of the federal government. Six of the ratifying states had proposed amendments that would protect individual rights in the face of such power, and anti-Federalists were threatening to convene a new constitutional convention. Madison, one of the framers of the Constitution, felt he could best protect the Constitution by changing it. Drawing inspiration from several state bills of rights, including those of his native Virginia, he submitted a set of nine protective amendments to Congress. These, he hoped, would both defend personal freedom and, at the same time, placate the most outspoken critics of the Constitution. Eventually Congress supported twelve amendments, and sent them off to the states for approval. Only ten were ratified, and these became, in December 1791, the Bill of Rights.

At four hundred words, the document is brief but far-reaching in its guarantees of personal liberties in America: freedom of speech, the press, religion, assembly, protection from unreasonable search and seizure, protection from cruel and unusual punishment. Americans cannot be forced to testify against themselves in criminal cases. One accused of a crime has the right to a speedy and public trial.

But for all its clarity, the Bill of Rights is a fluid document, one that has been interpreted anew by each successive generation. The Second Amendment's language—"A well regulated Militia, being necessary to the security of a free State, the right of the people to keep and bear Arms, shall not be infringed."—has fueled arguments on both sides of the gun control battle of the late twentieth century. Meanwhile, the Third Amendment's guarantee that "no Soldier shall, in time of peace, be quartered in any house, without the Consent of the Owner," is all but forgotten.

The Bill of Rights is also a somewhat limited document. Madison had proposed that "no state shall violate the equal rights of conscience, or the freedom of the press, or the trial by jury in criminal cases." But the Senate rejected this amendment so the Bill of Rights applied only to the federal government, not to the states. In the 1830s, the U.S. Supreme Court handed down a decision that confirmed this limitation. Thus, while the United States Congress could not pass laws limiting certain freedoms, state and local governments could, and routinely did. What's more, the freedoms outlined in the Bill of Rights were extended to a very limited part of the population. Women, children, American Indians, and men who owned no property received only limited protection from the Bill of Rights. Slaves had no rights whatsoever until the late 1860s, when the Constitution was again amended, this time to prohibit slavery and expand voting rights. The Fourteenth Amendment, which forbade the states limiting "the privileges or immunities of citizens," was also passed, but the courts interpreted this amendment very narrowly. Madison's dream of a nation freed from the "ambitious hope of making laws for the human mind" was far from being realized.

Throughout the nineteenth and into the twentieth century, state and local governments passed laws that flatly ignored the Bill of Rights. The federal government held that it could suspend all civil liberties in times of national crisis and the year 1917 proved to be just such a time. President Woodrow Wilson had won the presidential election the year before on a "peace and progressivism" platform and had pledged to keep the country out of the war in Europe. But in February, Germany announced its intention to continue its unrestricted submarine attacks on all ships at sea. Wilson abandoned his peace platform and broke off diplomatic relations with the German government. On April 2, he asked Congress for a declaration of war. On April 6, 1917, he got it.

It was a nervous America that prepared itself for battle. Pacifists and isolationists who had for months demanded that the U.S. stay neutral were now intimidated by the unbridled patriotism exhibited by the pro-war factions. The government's Committee on Public Information churned out propaganda promoting blind allegiance on the part of all. Dissent should not only be silenced, said the Committee, it should be punished. Former president Theodore Roosevelt called for vigorous police action against those speaking out against the war. He was not alone. American statesman Elihu Root, who had won the Nobel Peace Prize for championing the cause of international peace in 1912, now championed a rather ferocious form of patriotism instead. He told an audience in New York: "There are men walking about the streets of this city tonight who ought to be taken out at sunrise tomorrow and shot for treason." The audience cheered.

In very short order, Congress considered a raft of loyalty bills. One such piece of legislation, submitted by Senator George Chamberlain of Oregon, classified as a "spy" anyone who published anything "endangering the success of the military forces." Punishment could include the death penalty. Chamberlain's bill did not pass, but Attorney General Thomas Gregory had his office prepare more than a dozen loyalty proposals to deal with anti-war activity. Less than a month after war was declared, Gregory's office used the proposals to craft a single bill known as the Espionage Act. The bill would make it illegal for anyone to "willfully make or convey false reports or false statements with intent to interfere with the operation or success of the military or naval forces." Both Gregory and Wilson felt the law was a necessary symbolic gesture on the part of government, a rallying cry for a country newly-entered into war. But this proposed law was no mere rallying cry. One provision gave the postmaster general broad powers to determine as "unmailable" any materials deleterious to the war effort. Another set the punishment for breaking the law: "a fine of not more than $10,000 or imprisonment for not more than twenty years."

Proponents of the bill assured critics that there was no threat to freedom of speech. Congressmen Edwin Webb, who championed the bill in the House, said that government officials and army officers could be openly criticized, and that conditions in the armed forces could be freely discussed. The law was there to punish those few whose actions were dangerous to the nation, and to keep vital information from falling into the hands of the enemy.

There was, of course, considerable opposition to the Espionage Act; there was even vocal opposition to the war itself. In New York City alone there were a dozen or more peace organizations operating under such banners as the Committee for Democratic Control, the Women's Peace Party, the American Committee on War Finance, the National Peace Federation, and the World Peace Foundation. But these were groups with tiny memberships. As many as four of the organizations shared the same one-room office in Manhattan, and several people held positions in more than one of the groups.

The American Union Against Militarism was one of the larger, better-known pacifist organizations. Founded in 1915 to contest the call for U.S. "military preparedness," the AUAM, which changed its name several times during its seven-year history, had as its members some of the most committed and influential social reformers of the day: Lillian Wald of the Henry Street Settlement in New York; Jane Addams from Hull House in Chicago; labor activist Florence Kelley; Presbyterian minister and activist Norman Thomas; and Crystal Eastman, the author of New York State's first workers' compensation law. This was a group concerned with the social effects of war. Jane Addams told

readers of the *New York Evening Post* that "all the social gains of
the past" would be wiped out if America entered the war in
Europe. Public health, education reform, and labor and industrial
improvements were at risk. Democracy itself was threatened
when a nation went to war. "If a democracy is to go to war it
should go by direct mandate of the people through a referendum," wrote Crystal Eastman.

Within twelve months of its founding, the Union emerged as
the leading peace group, claiming upwards of two thousand
members and representatives in several major cities. Its aims
were simply stated: stop America from arming itself, stop the
arms industry from making a huge profit, and stop all conflict by
means of "popular diplomacy."

The AUAM could claim one prior success. In 1916, when
Mexican and American troops clashed at Carrizal, the AUAM
ran a massive publicity campaign to prevent a war with Mexico.
This pressure led to an unofficial mediation effort on the part
of Mexican and American pacifists and labor groups, a model of
the "popular diplomacy" the AUAM espoused. Under pressure,
President Wilson appointed a Joint High Commission on
Mexico. War was averted, and the Union proclaimed victory.
But public opinion was working against them on their fight to
stop military buildup against Germany, and leaders at the
AUAM knew they had little chance of stopping America's
entry into the conflict. Once war was declared, the more mod-
erate members of the AUAM felt that they should keep on
friendly terms with the U.S. government. Lillian Wald wanted
the group to turn its attention to the eventual peace negotia-
tions. She did not wish to be part of "a party of opposition to
the government" by protesting the Espionage Act, or the Selective Service Act, or any of the other pieces of military legislation being passed by a wartime Congress. But the more radical
members, led by Crystal Eastman, disagreed. "If as the war goes

on, it become more and more the deliberate intention of the government to militarize this nation.... The American Union Against Militarism must become, deliberately and obviously, the focus of the opposition," Eastman wrote.

Crystal Eastman surprised no one in her determination to steer the group toward opposition to war. She was herself a "deliberate and obvious" woman, a spirited and outspoken reformer with a sociology degree from Columbia and a law degree from New York University. As an early labor activist, she exposed the shocking lack of safety for industrial workers and as a suffragist she espoused "votes for all, special treatment for none." An early feminist, she agitated for free birth control, and urged women to take up "short hair and short skirts" as a step toward liberation. She was a founding member of the Women's Peace Party and a delegate to countless national and international peace conferences. At thirty-six, she was at the helm of the AUAM; she was also pregnant. She left the AUAM only briefly to have her baby, taking just a few weeks off in March 1917. Her executive position was left vacant, but her informal replacement was thirty-two-year-old Roger Baldwin, a social worker who had left a job in St. Louis to come work for the AUAM.

Roger Baldwin was, at the time, an avowed civil libertarian with what he described as "deep anarchist leanings." But an observer described him as "an offstage man ... adept at the wire-pullings, running of meetings, the enlisting of experts, the Machiavellisms that only fellow professionals can adequately appreciate." He was, then, a political man who could inspire and manipulate and a practical idealist who could work within the system for an unpopular cause. The AUAM job seemed perfect for him. Those who knew him well said that it was a job he had been born to.

The Baldwins of Massachusetts claimed at least two ancestors on the Mayflower, a coat of arms, and an apple. A Colonel Baldwin from Wilmington, Massachusetts, started the Baldwin orchards before 1750. The resultant Baldwin apple, "crisp, coarse, and juicy, with a spicy character..." was the perfect symbol for Roger Baldwin himself.

From his boyhood, Roger Baldwin exhibited the paradoxical mixture of character traits that defined him. Born into a wealthy Massachusetts shoe manufacturing family in 1884, Baldwin claimed to be a country boy. "My family kept pigs, sheep, cows, and horses." Of course his family also kept "a coachman, cook, gardener, parlormaid, nurse, and laundress." The Baldwin house in Wellesley, Massachusetts, was large and comfortable, with grounds that included a kitchen garden, a barn, five acres of pasture, and a pine forest. Throughout his life, Baldwin would recall his early years in Wellesley as idyllic. "I was an explorer, I was a hunter, not of the conventional kind, but a bird watcher, and a nature lover," he told one interviewer. "All my life, ever since that time, right up to now, I've been more attracted to the out of doors, and out of doors in the wilder places, than I am to any city."

Young Roger had ample opportunity to enjoy not only the natural world, but also the cultural amenities available to children of the well-to-do living around Boston. "I never heard my parents discuss money," he said. Even with six children, there was always money enough for excursions into Boston and summers on the South Shore. Roger was given music lessons, art lessons, dance lessons, and, as a teen, tickets for the Friday afternoon concerts at the Boston Symphony and the opera. "If I was conscious of the 'better people' it was only to know I was one of them," he said.

To be "one of them" meant more than having money. It meant attending the right church. For the Baldwins, this was the nearby Unitarian Society. "The servants went to the Catholic Church," he explained. If the Unitarian Society confirmed his place in the social register, it also helped the young man find his place in the world, for it was here that he displayed his earliest inclination toward social work. He assisted at Sunday school and he enlisted in the "Lend a Hand" club. He was a joiner and a good student to boot—he did well in every subject at school; he only did poorly in sports. By the time he was ready for college, he was known to be intelligent, conscientious, and marvelously well-rounded. As he said himself, "Harvard was quite inevitable."

"Boston society, the most oligarchical society in America, has the controlling vote in Harvard undergraduate society," wrote literary critic Van Wyck Brooks during Baldwin's college years. "Students who are not, to some extent, known and approved in Boston have some initial difficulty in making themselves known and approved in Cambridge." Needless to say, Roger Baldwin quickly found himself known and approved of quickly in his Harvard career. Every student committee and fraternal organization was open to him, but he eschewed the "snob" social clubs for the Musical Society and the Nature History Club. He also sought out the school's Social Service Committee at Phillips Brooks House, a sort of charity clearinghouse that was, as college president Eliot Norton said, "a benevolent association without parallel in the history of education." Concerned students—in Baldwin's time at Harvard this ran to over three hundred students a year—were assigned to all sorts of charity programs in the city of Boston. Young men donated their time ministering to the sailors at Boston's wharf, running the Sir Galahad Social and Athletic Club for the children of the poor, or distributing coal to needy families during the winter. In his first year on the Social Service Committee, Baldwin taught piano at a community center. The following year he became a recruiter for the group and convinced dozens of other Harvard students to join in the work.

Baldwin was not alone in the sense of duty he felt during his college years. He was part of a trend toward social consciousness that was arising in young men of education and privilege in America. Van Wyck Brooks wrote that college life had ceased "to be care-free, irresponsible, or impressionable, and becomes self-conscious, deliberate, and immoderately mature." Baldwin's step-son, Carl Baldwin, felt that this social concern was tied to Baldwin's social class and to his school. "There was a kind of upper-class understanding," he said. "Roger and his friends were all Harvard men. If you're from that background it's understood that you want to do some good, you want to make a contribution, you want to help your fellow man, you want to improve the world, maybe save the world."

"I liked society so much," Roger Baldwin said once, "that I was certain democracy would perfect it, and that good people, like us, could hasten this triumph." He was an optimist, a young man of social faith who continually sought out good people. One of them, future Supreme Court Justice Louis Brandeis, advised the young Baldwin to take up social work. It was a profession still in the making—there were no rigid standards in the profession, no limits on what an eager young man could take on in such a field. By the time he graduated from Harvard in 1905 with a B.A. and an M.A. in social science, Baldwin had decided that social work would be his future. With his aunt, Ruth Standish Baldwin, he traveled to New York City on a sort of grand tour, visiting the New York luminaries of the reform world: Jacob Riis, Lillian Wald, Owen Lovejoy, and Felix Adler. Baldwin called them "bright and busy saviors," and headed for a social work job in St. Louis, "full of uplift and confidence."

One writer has said of this period that Baldwin "liked living in St. Louis, where being a Baldwin did not count." This may be true, but what Baldwin seemed to really like about St. Louis was its size. St. Louis was a small pond, and he was able, in a few short years, to become a very big fish. He started out, in 1906, as the director of the Self Culture Hall settlement house, and simultaneously took on a volunteer position as an officer of the juvenile court. Within two years, his court job became official. He was the chief probation officer, and quickly developed an expertise on the juvenile justice system. He taught courses at Washington University, published articles in the *Ethical Culture Quarterly*, and accepted his first national office: secretary of the National Probation Association. During this time he took on the guardianship of two teenage boys, both sons of prostitutes, both of whom lived with Baldwin for short periods of time. In later life, Baldwin would speak fondly of these boys, Toto Stoltz and Oral James, but in fact he seemed to have some ambivalence about raising teenagers. Toto, Baldwin once said, "always called me Mr. Baldwin, and I never urged him to change." Both boys died in early manhood.

In 1910, Baldwin left the court system to become executive secretary of the St. Louis Civic League, a highly respected citizen's group supported, as Baldwin put it, "by all the best people." He encouraged the group to enlarge its charitable horizons to include the cause of popular control of government, and within a year was running a campaign to allow citizen initiatives to be placed on the ballot, voted on, and made into law. The campaign succeeded all too well. The good citizens of St. Louis used their newly-gained power to introduce and pass an initiative mandating that white and Negro citizens live in strictly segregated neighborhoods. The law, which was challenged in court and taken off the books, took the shine off of Baldwin's popular democratic idealism. "My too-simple theory of democracy had to be changed," he said. Indeed. At twenty-five, the young man had had his first lesson in the tyranny of the majority—strong medicine that somehow fortified his resolve to work for a better society. He was further strengthened by the preaching of the fiery anarchist, Emma Goldman.

Goldman was a known radical with an arrest record that dated back to 1893. She, along with fellow anarchist Alex Berkman, published *Mother Earth* and *The Blast*, pro-labor, pro-Bolshevik newspapers that earned her the title of "Red Queen." Russian-born, she was poor as the proverbial church mouse, and often had to suspend her political efforts so that she could earn money through private duty nursing. Baldwin, by his own report, was uninterested in her brand of politics. He went to hear her speak in 1909 in a working class hall in St. Louis because a friend goaded him into it. But her effect on him was immediate and lasting. "I was electrified the moment she opened her mouth," he said. "I became a revolutionist." After that speech he pulled a few strings with an influential publisher and got to meet Goldman face to face. He was intimidated by her self-taught brilliance and her feverish dedication to the unpopular cause of justice through anarchy. Goldman was not similarly impressed with him; she considered this upper-crust social worker to be a playboy surrounded by society girls. But the playboy pursued the anarchist. He arranged for Goldman to lunch with a group of powerful journalists, then landed her a respectable speaking engagement at a smart St. Louis women's club. Under her tutelage, he embarked on a period of serious study of anarchy and libertarianism. He read Prince Kropotkin's works, engaged in study group discussions, and, although he never gave himself the label of "anarchist," he admitted to being deeply tantalized by Goldman's vision of a "society so good... it didn't need governments to hold it together."

Baldwin managed to do all this and still hold onto his place in society. "I did not suffer from my sponsorship of Emma Goldman," he remembered. "It was regarded as an interesting philosophical excursion natural to a reformer and sociologist—and I saw to it that I had plenty of 'respectable' company." Nor did St. Louis society bristle when, in 1912, Baldwin sponsored another radical, birth control advocate Margaret Sanger. She had been barred by the police from delivering a birth control lecture in a private hall in St. Louis. Baldwin contacted her, and together they planned and held a small protest on the sidewalk outside the hall. Sanger spoke briefly, attracted a small crowd, and garnered what Baldwin called "excellent copy" in the press. After this, birth control lectures were permitted in St. Louis. Baldwin had staged his first free speech protest, and had won his first free speech battle.

In his St. Louis years, Baldwin proved that his willingness to learn had not stopped when he left college. His influences came from the world of radical thinkers, reformers, and labor organizers. He read works by Goldman, Sanger, and Jane Addams, and studied the work of "Big Bill" Haywood, the former copper miner who had founded the International Workers of the World in 1905. Baldwin was also attracted to pacifism. In 1914, when war broke out in Europe, he learned as much as he could about the men in Britain who refused to serve in the army there. This was his introduction to the conscientious objector. Baldwin admired these "high-minded young Englishmen going off to jail." He said they put him in mind of the peacemakers in the Sermon on the Mount. He was creating a personal philosophy and, at the same time, honing his considerable gift of persuasion. He became adept at calling the strategic meeting and firing off the pithy press release. He learned the value of the finely-timed protest, and, although he very much enjoyed the respect of the politically powerful, he had backbone enough to defy them when the popular stance ran contrary to his own. In 1917, when a Harvard friend asked Baldwin to support President Wilson's preparations for war, Baldwin declined. "I am

thoroughly with...the pacifists now and all the time," he
wrote. Indeed, within a few weeks of writing this letter he accepted a job as a secretary of the American Union Against
Militarism. In March he headed for New York, and on his own
terms: he would accept no salary, and he would serve only for
the duration of the war.

Chapter 2

Patriotic Fever:
Civil Liberties During World War I

We were in a period of intense majoritarian repression. If you didn't support the war patriotically, 100 percent, you were an enemy. And you were treated like an enemy.
—Burt Neuborne

Roger Baldwin arrived in New York in time for the declaration of war that came on April 6, 1917. He was, by his own admission, caught off guard, not by the declaration but by its effect on the American people. "I was very naive," he said. "I couldn't believe it would instantly produce such savage attitudes.... A sudden sort of hysteria happened very quickly." But Baldwin was not altogether naive. He realized almost at once that there would probably be a universal conscription law, compelling men to serve against their will. One of his first actions at the AUAM was to argue that the Union efforts would best be spent trying to influence this draft law, to somehow soften its impact. The board agreed, and immediately made Baldwin the associate director in charge of lobbying Washington for a "liberal bill that would not force men to fight."

In a way, the Union was not entirely unrealistic about these hopes for a liberal draft bill. President Wilson himself had said he hoped the bill could make allowances for men of conscience who could not bring themselves to fight. Wilson's secretary of war, Newton D. Baker, was a known progressive, a member of the League to Limit Armaments, and, for a time, an opponent to an all-out draft. Two months before war was declared, he had told President Wilson that "there would be great suspicion aroused if compulsory military service were suggested at the outset and before any opportunity to volunteer had been given." Baker thought he could raise an adequate army by mobilizing the National Guard, then issuing a call for volunteers. Such an army would be more democratic, more spirited, more American, and more willing to fight.

But fate, in the form of the blustering patriot and former president, Teddy Roosevelt, stepped in to change Baker's mind. The old Rough Rider applied for permission to raise an all-volunteer division and to personally command it on the battlefields of France. "I am a retired commander in chief of the United States Army and eligible to any position of command over American troops to which I may be appointed," he telegrammed Baker. The image of Roosevelt in charge of thousands of essentially untrained soldiers horrified Baker. He sent the telegram on to Wilson, who called it one of the "most extraordinary documents I've ever read." Wilson and Baker both politely refused Roosevelt's request. Roosevelt, furious, bombarded Congress and the White House with requests, then demands, that he be allowed to raise his division. Baker repeatedly said no, and announced that he would be asking Congress for swift enactment of a universal draft law.

Conscription was not a popular idea in America in 1917. "The volunteer system will give us a buoyant, determined, intrepid army," said one lawmaker. "Conscription is another word for slavery." White southerners were worried that a universal law would result in the arming of blacks. Industrialists complained that a draft would sap American factories of the best men. And many people remembered the Civil War, when, in 1863, Union soldiers on horseback rode forth to summon all able-bodied men to register for the draft. The men responded by rioting. In New York City, angry crowds sacked army and newspaper offices, then set fire to police stations. Blacks, who were seen as the cause of the war, were stoned, beaten, and hanged. A mob wielding weapons held firemen at bay while the Negro Orphan Asylum was burned to the ground. Secretary of War Stanton was hung in effigy from a 46th Street lamppost; the mangled corpse of an army officer dangled nearby. Three hundred people died in one day's rioting. Opponents of the draft predicted that America would relive this nightmare in 1917. Baker disagreed. He planned to give control of the draft to local election officials instead of the army. Local management would make conscription less heavy-handed and more acceptable to resistant Americans. He spent the better part of April crafting a piece of draft legislation that the country could live with.

Guided by Baldwin, the AUAM opposed military draft legislation. When it was clear that a draft law was inevitable, they tried to influence it. Four AUAM board members—Jane Addams, Lillian Wald, Emily Balch, and Norman Thomas— went to see President Wilson personally to make their concerns known. They could support a draft law only if it made allowances for every type of conscientious objector. They wanted a law that would make provisions for religious men who asked to be fully exempted from any war activity. They also urged consideration for objectors who were willing to serve in the army but not wear uniforms, for men who would wear uniforms but not enter a combat zone, and for men who would enter a combat zone but not carry a gun. They also hoped that the law that would accommodate political conscientious objectors— German-Americans, for example, who might not wish to fight their former countrymen, or Irish-Americans who would not care to serve alongside the British. They urged the secretary to use common sense in creating the draft. "Mennonite farmers are more useful in war times raising wheat than are the same young men dead or in prison," said Norman Thomas.

In the end, Baker disregarded the AUAM entirely. He submitted a bill to Congress that allowed exemptions only for members of "well-recognized religions and sects." The bill went on to say that "no person so exempted shall be exempted from service in any capacity that the President shall declare to be noncombatant." The bill flatly ignored political objectors, and made no provisions for absolutists. It passed both houses, although there was considerable debate in the Senate when Ohio's senator, Warren G. Harding, submitted an amendment that would allow Teddy Roosevelt to raise his volunteer division. That amendment failed, and Wilson signed the bill into law on May 18, 1917. The president sought to defuse all debate by saying that the draft "was in no sense a conscription of the unwilling, but rather selection from a nation which has volunteered in mass."

On registration day, June 5, 1917, 9,660,000 men of service age enlisted. There were no riots. Lucille Milner, who later worked for the ACLU, described registration day in St. Louis. "On the sidewalk outside was a long line of men waiting to register," she wrote. "Policemen and members of the Home Defense League . . . guarded the door. Boy scouts were there to assist. The crowd on the street . . . was lighthearted and good-humored."

Baldwin was not deterred in his efforts to secure government consideration for men unwilling to serve in the army. He set up a new committee within the AUAM: the Board for Conscientious Objectors. He contacted Secretary Baker and offered to help the War Department establish a policy for handling COs. To his delight, Baker accepted, and for weeks Baldwin split his time between New York and Washington, D.C., working with the AUAM board members to refine the recommendations, then lobbying the War Department to see that the recommendations were heeded. Baldwin drew up an extensive plan for handling COs, and blanketed Washington with copies of it. Even the president read the plan. Baldwin's Board attracted attention across the country. "We became known," he said.

Perhaps too much so. Lillian Wald and a few other board members, uncomfortable with the activist approach Baldwin was taking, threatened to quit the AUAM, and Crystal Eastman was the head of a house divided against itself. She attempted to placate Wald by having Baldwin's Board become a completely independent agency, with a slightly less radical name: the National Civil Liberties Bureau. The changes did no good, however. Wald made good on her threat to leave, and Eastman found herself off to the side of the movement that she had once spearheaded. Baldwin was front and center and just getting started. He did not wait for men to come to the NCLB for help; he collected the names of COs from religious and political newsletters and wrote to the men directly, offering them advice and legal support. The NCLB handled over one hundred CO cases each week. Baldwin found lawyers to represent them, raised defense funds from sympathetic donors in New York, and publicized the issues of war and conscience in a steady stream of letters, memos, and press releases.

To Roger Baldwin, the plight of the conscientious objector was the most important issue of the war. To Secretary Newton Baker, the CO question was chiefly a nuisance. He devoted his time to raising the army and in the early months of the war simply dragged his heels on the issue altogether; he seemed to wish it would go away. In August, when the first draftees began to report to camps for duty, there was still no real policy for handling COs. "After the conscientious objectors have been gotten into the camps and have made known their inability to proceed with military work, their number will be ascertained and a suitable work evolved for them," Baker said. He traveled to Camp Meade in September 1917 to see firsthand how this non-policy would work. "Out of eighteen thousand men there appeared twenty-seven... objectors," he reported to Wilson. These included "nine Old Amish, two New Amish, three Friends," and a number of men belonging to little-known churches, including the Brothers of God and the Assembly of God. One man, Baker noted, was a Russian-born Jew who claimed to be an International Socialist. "I think," reported Baker, "he is simply lazy and obstinate, without the least comprehension of International Socialism." While Baker was at Meade, one of the COs had watched the soldiers playing football and baseball, then withdrawn his objection and joined in the games. Baker took much comfort in this one man's change of heart. "My belief," he wrote the president, "is that we ought to proceed."

But by simply proceeding with no real plan, Baker put enormous power in the hands of local draft officials and army camp commanders, men who, for the most part, had little sympathy for the CO, and none for the absolutists who refused to do any war-related work. "The government turned them [the absolutists] over to the local tribunals, who have made a ludicrous mess of it, as of most else they have touched," wrote one observer in the *Living Age*. "The treatment of the unexempted CO has, with wide and illogical variation, been brutal and stupid." Norman Thomas's brother, Evan, was jailed as a CO and for a period of weeks spent eight hours a day manacled to the bars of his cell. Thomas read his brother's letters aloud in the NCLB office.

Throughout the war, the NCLB received hundreds of such letters from men describing their ordeals: they were beaten, their heads were forced into filthy latrines, they were dragged by ropes, and they were held in solitary confinement for weeks.

Baldwin and the NCLB staff were outraged by such treatment, but the public at large felt only antipathy for men who refused to go to war. "My son," wrote Leonard Ely Quigg in the *New York Tribune*, "my only child, in prompt response to his country's duly sounded call is today headed for the French trenches, there to be the target of German bullets. The mouth of sedition should be shut by a bullet."

Throughout 1917, Baldwin kept up his lobbying on behalf of COs at the War Department. He also became a familiar face at the Justice Department, where he met with officials to discuss the growing number of civil liberties problems stemming from the Espionage Act. The post office became Baldwin's chief bugbear. Postmaster General Albert Burleson exercised his power of virtual censorship with a heavy hand. In June, for example, Burleson ruled that the Socialist magazine, the *Masses*, contained seditious material and was therefore unmailable. Then, because the issue was not mailed, Burleson revoked the publication's second class mailing privileges, saying it was not in compliance with postal regulations. This loss of privileges effectively put the magazine out of business. The NCLB protested directly to the White House, but President Wilson considered Burleson one of his most reliable advisors and he let the decision stand.

Burleson recast the postal system into a national intelligence network during World War I. He told every postmaster in the country to report any materials remotely "questionable" to Washington. He routinely revoked mailing privileges, and suppressed hundreds of documents, including more than a dozen of the NCLB publications. "The post office," said Baldwin, "became a graveyard for us."

Support for the Espionage Act grew as American troops entered the battles in France. A writer in the *New York World* observed, "if there ever was a time when treason deserved to be punished as treason that time has come, and the longer we delay

the deeper this cancer will eat into the vitals of the Republic."
States and cities passed their own versions of the Espionage Act,
many of them aimed at curbing the radical political and labor
groups that had sprung up in the years before the war. Arrests for
even the slightest offenses became common. One group of farmers in South Dakota were arrested and jailed for signing a petition that called the conflict a "capitalist's war." Constitutional
scholar Zechariah Chafee Jr., cautioned against such extreme enforcement of the Espionage Act; such convictions, he said,
"make practically all opposition to the war criminal."

Americans joined dozens of private and government-sponsored
organizations that existed partly to boost the war effort, partly to
spy on their neighbors. Attorney General Gregory boasted that
he had "hundreds of citizens...keeping an eye on disloyal individuals and making reports on disloyal utterances." The American Patriotic League, the American Defense Society, and the
National Security League all included private citizens who were
deputized as loyalty agents. The American Patriotic League even
gave its members "Secret Service" identity cards. At one point,
several of these APL men visited Baldwin, looking for information on the NCLB. When he found out who they were, he
promptly threw them out. "This wartime job was high tension,
perpetual pressure," he said. "And I took to it almost with a feeling of elation." The NCLB's nervous landlord did not share the
enthusiasm. Anticipating trouble, he ordered them to move.

Even an eviction did not stop Baldwin's campaign on behalf
of pacifism. His opposite number in the government, George
Creel, chairman of the Committee on Public Information,
headed what was described by one observer as a "gargantuan advertising agency." If Baldwin's job was to sell the idea that conscience had a place in a nation at war, Creel's job was to sell
blind loyalty for every part of the war effort: the draft, the food
rationing, the seizure of railroads, the selling of war bonds, and

the abridgement of freedom of speech and the press. Creel, forty-one, was a journalist of sorts, a newspaperman from Missouri whose free-ranging career covered virtually every sector of American publishing. He had worked as a reporter in Kansas City, New York, and Denver. He had also worked as a joke writer and songwriter. He published his own inspirational books, edited his own magazine, and entered the political arena as a tireless campaigner for Wilson, who rewarded him with the chairmanship of the CPI. Like Baldwin, Creel relied heavily on newspapers to publicize his cause. Unlike Baldwin, Creel expected that the press releases coming out of the CPI would be printed word for word. "Why not?" he asked. "Newspaper men, it must be remembered, [were] holding peacetime jobs while others sacrificed or fought." Creel was as skilled and dynamic as Baldwin, and he had virtually unlimited resources at hand. His Division of News was *the* source for war information; his *Official Bulletin* was displayed in every post office in the country; and his speakers' bureau, featuring the "Four Minute Men," gave countless lectures across the country. Creel had thousands of feet of film footage taken by the Signal Corps to package and distribute to the film-news weeklies. One such film piece, dated July 20, 1917, shows Secretary Baker, in formal dress, blindfolded. Before him is a glass jar containing 10,500 numbers on folded slips of paper. This was the drawing for "the first great draft lottery." In the footage Creel released to the theaters, Baker draws the number 258, which is written on a placard—men holding the number 258 will be the first to report to army camp. The footage then shows a large crowd of draft age men, some of them presumably holding the draft number 258. They cheer wildly, and, reportedly, audiences in the theaters cheered along.

Baldwin, by contrast, had no film footage, no speakers' bureau, no insider's access to information. He had a one-room office, a typewriter, a stenographer, and a few part-time associates.

Nonetheless, he made the NCLB a prominent voice for individual rights at a time when it was unpopular, and, in fact, dangerous, to speak out against the war. District attorneys across the country brought hundreds of cases under the Espionage Act in 1918, and in case after case, the courts handed down the maximum sentence of ten years. Baldwin thrived on this atmosphere of risk and on his role as gadfly and outsider. Carl Baldwin remembered that Roger "always felt a kind of kinship with nonconformists that goes back to his early Boston days. He identified with Henry David Thoreau's writing on civil disobedience. And he identified with Eugene Debs."

Eugene V. Debs was a union organizer, a founder of the Socialist Party of America. He was a perennial presidential candidate on the Socialist ticket; in the 1912 election, he had received almost one million votes. Baldwin, not being a socialist, had not been very interested in Debs. Then, in 1918, Debs was arrested for making an impassioned anti-war speech at a rally in Cleveland. Baldwin protested and followed the case closely. Debs was charged with three counts of violating the Espionage Act. At his trial he told the judge, "I would not take back a word of what I believe right to save myself from the penitentiary." Debs's stirring words inspired Baldwin; Debs's sentence, ten years in prison, infuriated him. Debs's stiff jail term sent an alarming signal to the NCLB—they realized that the Bureau was treading a dangerous path and that the board and the staff could very well be arrested for their work with men avoiding the draft. Baldwin proceeded cautiously in his advisory work. He did not proselytize and he did not encourage men to resist the draft. He claimed that he was "scrupulously careful" in giving out advice. But he also admitted that, under the Espionage Act, the very existence of the NCLB could be seen as illegal. And as the war progressed, officials in the War Department agreed. Baldwin was told that his advice was no longer welcome in the nation's capitol and he and the NCLB

board steeled themselves against an expected espionage indictment. None was forthcoming, perhaps because there were so
many other groups that the government was watching. "There
were pacifists, there were socialists, there were communists, there
were Wobblies—members of the International Workers of the
World," says Anthony Lewis, noted legal writer. "All sorts of organizations, all with tiny memberships, that ambitious politicians
focused on as dangers to our way of life."

The IWW was seen as a particularly dangerous organization.
The union was small, but notorious. "Big Bill" Haywood had garnered headlines since the union's founding, delivering stirring
speeches about the IWW's aim of "emancipation for all workers
from the thrall of capitalism." Haywood gained further notoriety
in 1907, when he and some other western labor leaders were tried
and acquitted for the murder of a former governor of Idaho. Since
that time he had kept himself in the forefront of every labor
struggle, and had taken over the official leadership of the IWW
in 1914. He and his fellow IWW members, often called "Wobblies," were hounded by state and federal agents throughout the
war. In October 1917, 166 members of the union were charged
with sedition and held without bail in Chicago. Federal agents
ransacked their union hall. When the IWW set up a defense
team, agents raided the defense offices. The post office tampered
with their mail, delaying delivery, and, in a few cases, "losing"
checks being sent out by the legal committee.

At this point, Baldwin offered to help. He wrote the White
House, asking the president to intervene, but Wilson would not.
So Baldwin set about raising defense funds, and had the NCLB
produce a pamphlet, "The Truth about the IWW," a pains-
takingly researched publication that cleared the IWW of any
anti-war activity. Burleson pronounced it "unmailable," and
federal agents pressured shipping companies not to carry it.
American Patriotic League volunteers trailed IWW Defense

Committee members who attempted to mail small packets of the pamphlets at various post offices throughout Chicago. The cat-and-mouse game escalated when the NCLB tried to place a pro-IWW advertisement in the *New Republic*. Government agents "encouraged" the magazine to reject the ad. It did.

Meanwhile, Congress was considering the Walsh Bill, a piece of legislation that would outlaw the IWW entirely. Baldwin found the bill to be crushingly repressive and dangerously vague, one that could have a deadening effect on all organized labor. The sponsor, Senator Thomas Walsh, introduced the bill saying that "he did not regard the IWW fellows as representatives of the laboring class...I regard them...as public enemies." It passed easily in the Senate, and seemed likely to pass in the House as well, until one congressman slowed the process by calling for hearings. The White House made it known that Wilson did not support the bill, and it died quietly. Baldwin took this as an encouraging sign. In April 1918, he traveled to Chicago for the IWW trial in a hopeful frame of mind. But the IWW leader Bill Haywood and ninety-six of his co-defendants were found guilty of anti-war crimes. Haywood was fined thirty thousand dollars and sentenced to twenty years in prison. Haywood posted bail and spent the remainder of the war years appealing the conviction.

By late summer 1918, Roger Baldwin had made himself entirely unwelcome in Washington. One of Baker's assistants wrote him that "in this hour when every good citizen is devoting himself...to further the interests of his country, gentlemen of your undoubted talents and ability might find better employment than that of directing your efforts and energies toward the protection of men who—we cannot blink at the fact—are essentially enemies of your country." His "approval rating" was probably at an all-time low with the War Department. Nonetheless, the army wanted Roger Baldwin. A change in the draft law in August made unmarried men up to the age of forty eligible. Baldwin, thirty-four, resigned his post at the NCLB, turned the office over to an associate, attorney Albert DeSilver, and stayed home to see what would happen next. The NCLB office was then raided by the Justice Department and its files, including Baldwin's personal papers, were removed. When DeSilver protested, one of the agents drew a revolver. DeSilver stepped aside, and the agents made off with the files.

Twelve days later, on September 12, Baldwin received his draft notice. He posted a "polite refusal" to his draft board, and sent a copy to the district attorney's office. On October 11 he was arrested at home, taken before the draft board, and given a chance to change his mind. "I am not an absolutist," he said later, "but the government required every man of military age to become a soldier or a criminal, and the choice was inescapable." He would not recant, so the agents deposited him for the night in a New York City jail. The next morning, Baldwin was taken into custody by what he called several "hilarious" agents, one of whom promised Baldwin "the fanciest little arrest you've ever heard of." The agents took Baldwin out for a "bang-up breakfast" and a shave, then chauffeured him, by limousine, to Justice Department offices, where instead of a grueling interrogation, he was treated to a pleasant chat with the boys. But he refused to change his mind, and refused to post bail. The agents had no choice but to return him to jail. He was deposited at the Tombs to await trial. He spent his nights there, but spent his days at the Union League Club, where the seized NCLB files had been haphazardly stored. Baldwin was given the task of cleaning them up so that the Justice Department could study them for signs of treasonous activity. "The FBI treated me as a guest and often took me out to dinner and the theater," he recalled.

Baldwin's case was tried on October 30, 1918, in U.S. District

Court in New York City. He was surrounded by friends and well-wishers, and he received messages of support from almost his entire family, the one exception being his Uncle George, a stockbroker. His Aunt Ruth, who had first introduced him to the reformers a decade before, was in the courtroom during the trial. Baldwin freely admitted to the charges of resisting the draft, and requested no special treatment. "Whatever the penalty, I shall endure it," he said. What he would endure, ruled the judge, was one year in a civilian penitentiary. On Armistice Day, 1918, he was taken to the Essex County Jail in Newark, and thus commenced what could well have been the most pleasant, and was certainly the most unusual, prison term to come out of the CO experience during World War I.

Norman Siegel of the ACLU has said that "the fact that he went to jail in World War I, rather than serve in the military, I think really sums up Roger. Most of us have commitment, most of us have loyalties, but how many of us are really willing to go to jail?" Fortunately for Baldwin, jail was not that bad an experience. At Newark, says Carl Baldwin, "the warden was an Irish-American. He said to him, 'Mr. Baldwin, I don't like England's war either.' So there was a kind of camaraderie between the warden, who was anti-English, and Roger, who was just anti-government, anti-war. And he survived. I think the warden let him out to do gardening and stuff. He kind of had the run of the place. And he had a way of doing things like that. He was a charming guy, you know. If anybody could charm a warden, Roger could."

While Baldwin was charming the warden, Albert DeSilver ran the NCLB. But Baldwin kept close tabs on the office, and, in fact, kept his hand in the running of things, albeit at a distance. Alan Reitman, who later worked for Baldwin as the ACLU's publicist, explained that "the warden allowed him to leave the jail around noon, and on a bench in Military Park in Newark he

would meet with officials from the Bureau, and they would conduct...business. When lunchtime was over, Roger would go
back to jail and continue to serve his sentence."

In jail, Baldwin worked as a cook and a gardener. In a reprise
of his Lend-a-Hand club days, he organized a prisoner's welfare
league, a reading group, a glee club, and a dramatic society. As always, he enlisted the aid of "better people," including the
wealthy socialite, Mrs. Sidney Colgate, who adopted Baldwin as
a pet project. "We attracted the attention of some good ladies interested in prisons." But Baldwin also attracted the attention of
the county sheriff, who felt that far too good a time was being
had at public expense. He demanded that the reform activity
cease at once. Baldwin, of course, refused and fell back on his
usual tactics: he wrote the press and alerted the "good people."
Mrs. Colgate complained, the sheriff backed down, and the activities continued, but only until Baldwin, at his own request,
was transferred to the New Jersey prison farm at Caldwell.

Baldwin called his time at Caldwell a "vacation courtesy of
the government." He was on a first name basis with the guards
and with the liberal warden, who was, like Baldwin, a member
of the National Conference of Social Workers. He passed his
time there studying and working outdoors, getting in "better
physical shape" than he had been in years. When he learned
that, due to a clerical error, his sentence had been shortened by
one month, he wrote to the District Court: "I was sentenced to
this jail...for a term of eleven months and ten days. I find that
the commitment on file here reads 'ten months and eleven
days.'" But the error was not corrected, and in July 1919 Roger
Baldwin was a free man once again.

During his jail term, the surgeon general's office had issued the
results of a study showing that conscientious objectors were
something of a select group. They were not only significantly
more intelligent than men jailed for other offenses, they were

also more intelligent than most army officers. What's more, the COs were far less likely than the population as a whole to have been imprisoned for any crime prior to the war. "It does not seem likely," wrote Winthrop D. Lane, "that we need fear much from future criminal activity of the conscientious objector." Baldwin agreed. He remembered his fellow CO prisoners with fondness. "For two months or more I took every opportunity to go back and chat with the warden and guards and a few of the prisoners," he said later. "I felt an almost inexplicable attachment to the Caldwell Prison. It stayed with me in my dreams."

But prison, for most conscientious objectors, was not the stuff of dreams. In 1918 there were nearly five hundred men imprisoned at the U.S. Disciplinary Barracks, Fort Leavenworth, Kansas. The COs jailed here were under the jurisdiction of military commanders, many of whom saw COs as cowards and slackers. Ignoring the positive findings of the surgeon general's office, one army officer declared that these men, when released, would "make the worst possible kinds of criminals." Indeed, for many COs, the conditions of confinement were so horrific that they could well have become deeply bitter men, if not hardened criminals. Solitary confinement and bread and water diets were typical for the absolutists held in military prisons. Men who refused to work were manacled to the bars and forced to stand upright for eight hours a day. One group of prisoners, held at Camp Funston, were subjected to the "water cure," a tortuous sequence of forced marches followed by cold showers. One man wrote that he had been placed in irons, then put to hard labor. "Yesterday afternoon I worked with a shovel and a pick in the ditch with these hobbles on, but today they made it worse. They put me to carrying stone from 5 to 150 pounds weight.... Tonight my ankles are bruised and sore, but I lasted it out fine." Another CO wrote to the NCLB that he had been dragged by a rope around his neck until his skin peeled off. "They shaved my head, they cuts my ears. They put a saber to my neck. They tore my shirt in pieces and wanted me to put on a uniform. They threw me in an ice cold bath."

The War Department did not condone these practices, but it did little to prevent them. "The War Department can by no means escape blame," wrote Norman Thomas. "It was slow in investigating and slow in righting wrong."

After the Armistice in November 1918, DeSilver and the NCLB board pushed for legislation that would free all COs at once. Congress said no to a blanket amnesty and release policy, but the Wilson administration commuted sentences and sent many of the COs home. This infuriated some soldiers, since some COs were sent home before the army discharged its draftees. When the NCLB asked the government for a general amnesty for all those imprisoned under the Espionage Act, Wilson flatly refused. The convicted must serve out their terms, no matter how long those terms might be. The president, and the nation, would prove themselves very slow to forgive.

Chapter 3

Our Place Is
in the Fight:
The Founding of the ACLU

It's no accident that the ACLU came into being when it did after World War I. After all, the Wilsonian era increased the size and scope of government substantially, and it became much more authoritarian. When you look back on that period and you see some of the things that took place, it makes you wonder: was this America?

—Roger Pilon

When he got out of prison, Roger Baldwin didn't race back to civil liberties work. Instead, he raced to the altar to marry Madeline Doty, herself a civil libertarian and pacifist, a woman with a lengthy political resume of her own. Theirs was a no-frills wedding, held outdoors—no bridal dress, no tuxedo, no ring. They wrote their own vows: Baldwin, in his, said that "the present institution of marriage is a grim mockery of essential freedom." Doty was more traditional: "My one desire is that our love may increase your power to live." She did add that their marriage would be "a foundation for the new brotherhood of which we strive." Baldwin and Doty took a short trip to the Adirondacks. Then Baldwin set out on much longer trip alone.

For Baldwin, this trip was something of an experiment. He thought he might see what the less-privileged existence of the working man was like. So in the early fall 1919, he traveled to Chicago by train, with only a few dollars in his pocket. There, he picked up an IWW union card—Bill Haywood, the union leader, sponsored him. Planning to use his prison-acquired skills as chef, he also picked up an AFL union card from the Cooks and Waiters Union. The warden at the Caldwell prison in New Jersey served as his reference there. He then left Chicago, riding the rails, bumming for real. In St. Louis he visited old friends, upper-crust liberals from his social work days. The newspapers got wind of his visit, and made quite a story out of the former Civic League director's being a bum. The publicity, said Baldwin, was "unpleasant." He took his one suitcase and his two union cards and headed out of town.

For the next two months, Roger Baldwin got his wished-for taste of the working man's life. He worked in a brickyard for thirty-seven cents an hour, then found a job in a coalyard. These non-union jobs only lasted a few days each—he kept traveling, eager to find a job that would draw him into the thick of the labor struggle. He found such a job in Pittsburgh, where a major strike was going on at the Homestead Steel Mills. At the behest of a union official, Baldwin signed on as a scab; he was, in actuality, a union spy. By day, he cleaned the factory furnaces. His ten-hour shift over, he went back to his hotel room to make notes on the goings-on inside the plant. After a week he was fired with no reason given. That evening he found his room ransacked and his notes gone. He spent a nervous night, waiting to be arrested or worse, but although more than a dozen strikers were beaten that night by company thugs, he was not bothered. At dawn he made his way to the union hall, gave his report, and headed off to West Virginia, where martial law had been imposed after a coal strike. No job in West Virginia seemed as interesting as his union spying, and life on the road had worn thin. He had put in several weeks of back-breaking labor. He had even been hungry a few times. He drifted north, towards New York City, and made it home for Thanksgiving dinner.

Before he had left, some of Baldwin's friends had tried to talk him out of the trip. A Harvard man had no business trying to pass himself off as a common laborer. They were arguably right. Baldwin was dabbling. "Roger's a friend of the working man," Clarence Darrow once said. "That's a lot easier than being one." His life on the road was no more difficult than his life in prison. But in making this trip Baldwin showed his eagerness to learn about life firsthand, an eagerness that set him apart. He was, after all, probably the only man in his college class, and possibly the only man in his social class, who could lay claim to a Harvard diploma, an IWW card, and a felony conviction. "He was a maverick," said Burt Neuborne, former legal director of the ACLU. Chuck Morgan, a former ACLU attorney who met Baldwin in the 1960s, said that "Baldwin was a free roamer. He had a mind that ranged as far as the world would go."

Eighteen months of war had whetted the American appetite for peace and for a "return to normalcy." But there was no general agreement as to the meaning of this wished-for "normalcy." Baldwin and like-minded reformers wanted to revisit the Progressive Era and continue with their programs of education, health care, and worker safety. Industrialists, on the other hand, had had enough of reform and of labor unions. Meanwhile, the government canceled hundreds of military contracts, and nine million men lost their war industry jobs as a result. Surging inflation fed the growing labor unrest. "After World War I," said historian Mary McAuliffe, "you had a drained population. A population that had given its all to defeat a very powerful enemy. What did it have when it was through? More problems. More difficulties."

"And now what will become of us without the barbarians?" was a sentiment voiced in Greece after Alexander defeated the Persians. Americans in 1919 felt much the same way. They missed the German enemy that had united them in the patriotic cause of war. They needed a new enemy, and they found it. "The Bolshevik Revolution," said writer Anthony Lewis, "scared Americans out of their wits."

The Russian Revolution of 1917 was an upheaval on as grand a scale as the modern world had seen, and the Bolshevik goal of world domination by the proletariat was a terrifying prospect. Alan Reitman, who worked for Baldwin as ACLU publicity director in the late 1940s, remembered the anxiety that he and his family felt about the Russian Revolution in the 1920s. "There was a tremendous fear," he said. "We felt that what happened in Russia would somehow seep into our own country."

The popular press fed this fear. Readers of the *Saturday Evening Post* were told that the Bolshevik regime was "a compound of slaughter, confiscation, anarchy and universal disorder." But some American radicals, including many Wobblies, openly supported the Soviet Revolution. It gave them hope. If a system as firmly entrenched as Czarism in Russia could be toppled, could not a more mobile, democratic system like that of the U.S. be changed as well? In their enthusiasm, the left wing began to adopt the ideology and the slogans of the Russians. "All Power to the Soviet!" and "Workers Unite!" headlined the small but vocal mix of radical publications: *Novy Mir, Mother Earth*, the *Blast*, and *Obrana*.

In 1919, there were two American communist parties, both with tiny memberships. But this small political movement was quickly lumped with other American leftist movements: the Socialist Party, which had one hundred thousand members; the

IWW, with sixty thousand members; and the mainstream labor movements, with members numbering into the millions. Employers and industrialists found this confusion very useful in their efforts to stifle the labor movement. They contributed large sums to the National Civic Federation and the National Security League, then urged these patriotic groups to keep organized labor at the top of the enemy list.

Ironically, much of organized labor was itself anti-radical. During the war the AFL had put patriotism first, the needs of labor second. Samuel Gompers, president of the AFL, had been a speaker for the National Security League. "Let us ... see to it that Uncle Sam has the fighting men and the men to produce at home and the money with which to carry on the war. Let us defer questions which can be deferred, questions that are likely to divide us in this war. Let us remain united and fight it out, now matter how long we fight." In 1919, Gompers pledged that all AFL union organizing would be strictly American; the following year he refused to endorse a resolution calling for total amnesty for political prisoners, saying that most political prisoners were radicals. Gompers was not rewarded for such loyalty. Indeed, he and his four million AFL members were tarred with the same radical brush as the Wobblies and the Communists.

Fear of organized labor was fueled by several prominent labor actions in 1919. When the Iron and Steel Workers staged major strikes in Pennsylvania, the union and its striking members were routinely written up in the Pittsburgh press as "rioters," "foreigners," and "terrorists." The violent strike-breaking measures carried out by the state constabulary were suppressed by the newspapers, or reported in such a way that the reading public became convinced that the strike was anarchistic attempt to overthrow the state government. In one case, the *Chronicle–Telegraph* reported that state troopers had located an alleged sniper in his home and had shot him in self defense. Eyewitnesses reported that the man, Nicholas Gratachini, was sitting outdoors in broad daylight when a number of troopers stormed into the yard, firing shots. He was killed as he attempted to get back inside his house with his four-year-old niece in his arms.

Such reportage was not limited to the steel strike. The Mine Workers and the Boston police force also staged labor actions in 1919. The Boston police were striking for their right to join the AFL; President Wilson called it "a crime against civilization." The biggest attention grabber was in Seattle: a city-wide general strike that captured headlines and inspired terror across the country.

The Seattle strike started in January 1919 with thirty-five thousand shipyard workers demanding higher pay and shorter working hours. On February 3, Seattle's Central Labor Council— which included members of the AFL and the IWW—called for a general strike to begin in three days. Seattle citizens panicked and flocked to the stores to lay in food and medical supplies. Handguns sold at a brisk pace. Sixty thousand workers stayed home on February 6, and work in the city slowed to a crawl. The mayor, Ole Hanson, called in federal troops, and labor leaders, many of them under pressure from their international officers, agreed to stop the strike. "The rebellion is quelled," crowed Ole Hanson, "This Bolshevik-sired nightmare is over." No matter that the nightmare had lasted only four days, that milk had been delivered and garbage picked up throughout. No matter that there had been no violence. The unions were villains, the mayor was a hero. When it was over, the whole nation cheered. Hanson became so popular that he was able to leave his job and make a living on the loyalist stump circuit.

News of anti-union mob violence grew with each labor action. At the NCLB, Albert DeSilver received reports of fifty such cases, all of them involving attacks on the IWW. In one case in Centralia, Washington, when the mood of a patriotic parade turned ugly, townspeople decided to storm the IWW union hall.

Gunshots were exchanged, four men were killed, and the Wobblies fled the hall. The mob caught one man, then brutally murdered him. The coroner ruled the death a suicide. "The victim," the coroner wrote, "jumped off [a bridge] with a rope around his neck then shot himself full of holes."

It was in this period of violence and turmoil that Roger Baldwin walked back into the NCLB office in New York City to survey the damage. DeSilver had put much energy into lobbying Washington on behalf of those jailed under the Espionage Act. His attempts were unsuccessful and wildly unpopular. "People who are not for this government are against it, and should be either in prison or deported," wrote one man to the NCLB. "I would be opposed to any scheme to liberate them." The Bureau, for its efforts to win freedom for the prisoners, was called "un-American, unpatriotic and generally undesirable."

Baldwin announced that the organization must be changed. It must distance itself from the NCLB, with its image of working only with conscientious objectors. "Our place is in the fight," he wrote. "The cause we now serve is labor." The new organization needed a new board of directors and a new name that reflected this new cause. After considering several options, Baldwin settled on the American Civil Liberties Union. DeSilver would stay on as an associate. Baldwin was once again in charge.

"Baldwin came in and said 'we'll expand freedom and expand American democracy and make it better for everyone,'" said Chuck Morgan. "He was the heart that beat inside the ACLU during its early years." Baldwin was the heartbeat, the pulse, the brain, and the conscience of the new organization. He and DeSilver served as co-directors. There was a large executive committee and a smaller directing committee, but Baldwin, with the blessing of everyone involved, ran the show.

"We Will Dynamite You!" This from anarchist posters that appeared in the Northeast in 1919. "There will have to be bloodshed....We will kill. We will destroy." This from the anarchist newspaper, *Plain Words*. But there were more than words hurled about in spring 1919. In April, thirty-six hand-made bombs were mailed, in packages marked "Novelty—A Sample," to government officials around the nation. Several were duds. Several others were intercepted by the New York post office, where they were being held for insufficient postage. One exploded in the home of Senator Thomas W. Hardwick of Georgia, where two women were seriously injured. Hardwick's maid lost her hand and his wife was severely burned. "BEWARE OF PACKAGE IF IT COMES IN THE MAIL. DO NOT OPEN IT. CALL THE POLICE BOMB SQUAD." This from the *Chicago Tribune*. Many newspapers carried similar warnings, and across the country packages were routinely doused with water.

On June 2, 1919, bombs exploded in eight cities across the country. One of them went off on the doorstep of Attorney General A. Mitchell Palmer. "The blaze of revolution," said Palmer, "was sweeping over the American institution of law and order." The bombers, never caught, were assumed to be anarchists. Americans liberals and leftists loudly condemned them. A few people, including some in Baldwin's New York circle, thought the bombs could been planted by government agents to frame anarchists and stir up even more hatred of radicals.

Attorney General Palmer was a Quaker from Pennsylvania, a lawyer, and a Democrat who had worked hard on Woodrow Wilson's presidential campaign. Wilson had offered Palmer the position of secretary of war in 1913, but Palmer declined, saying, "I am a man of peace." As attorney general, his peaceful nature was sorely tested by the bombings. His first response was to set up a "General Intelligence Division" in the Department of Justice. At its head, Palmer placed a young bureaucrat, J. Edgar Hoover.

Hoover, who once worked at the Library of Congress, immediately launched a brilliant surveillance and records campaign. He soon had index cards—painstaking detailed and cross-referenced—on two hundred thousand people.

Congress wanted something stiffer than an investigation, and a flurry of postwar sedition bills were introduced. These bills would, variously, outlaw the flying of red flags, the exhibition of Soviet emblems, and the use of the German language in the U.S. mail. One bill would allow for the deportation of any alien convicted of any crime. Representative Kenneth D. McKellan of Tennessee suggested that native-born radicals be deported to a special penal colony in Guam. Palmer himself drafted a bill that made it illegal to "cause the change, overthrow or disturbance of the government." Illegal to change the government, or fly a red flag? As one critic pointed out, Harvard men could be arrested for flying their crimson banner. "I am a beginning farmer," joked one ACLU member from Mt. Kisco. "I have just been given six Rhode Island Reds; they are hens. Under the Espionage law is it safe for me to keep them?" But it was no joking matter to lawmakers in twenty states, who put anti-red flag laws on their books in 1919.

Even as he drafted his own version of a sedition bill, Palmer was planning more decisive moves against radicals. On November 7, 1919, the second anniversary of the Russian Revolution, Justice Department agents, under the direction of Hoover, raided the social halls of the Union of Russian Workers in a dozen cities. "The federal government," reported *The New York Times*, "aided by municipal police in New York and other cities, last night dealt the most serious and sweeping blow it has yet aimed at criminal anarchists." Eyewitnesses to the New York raid reported that the agents kicked in doors, tore apart furniture, and clubbed the people inside, many of whom were there to study English. Some were "badly beaten by police . . . their heads wrapped in bandages testi-

fying to the rough manner in which they had been handled."
Similar reports came in from Detroit; Philadelphia; Jackson,
Michigan; and Ansonia, Connecticut.

Palmer made an end run around the justice system by charging
the detainees with immigration violations instead of crimes. As
a result, most of those arrested never saw a judge or jury. More
than two hundred men were simply brought to Ellis Island to
await deportation. When a small number of wives and children
of the deportees attempted to join the men on Ellis Island, one
newspaper announced that "Reds Stormed Gates to Free Pals."
Using the administrative charges, the Justice Department and
the Department of Labor were able to deport two hundred men
taken in the URW raids. They were sent to the Soviet Union on
the *Buford*, the same ship that carried Baldwin's mentor, Emma
Goldman, into exile. Palmer promised that the citizens of New
York would see a "second, third, and fourth Soviet Ark sailing
down their beautiful harbor in the near future."

On January 2, 1920, the Justice Department struck again. In
what became known as the "Palmer raids," federal agents swept
up over four thousand radicals across the country, seizing people
without warrants and destroying personal property. People were
arrested for even looking foreign. Any alien who admitted to
being a member of the Communist Party was taken into custody.
Thousands were held without charges and were not permitted to
see either counsel or family. Hoover later denied the wide-spread
charges of mistreatment, but in Detroit, eight hundred people
were held in a windowless corridor for four days. One groups of
aliens, held for several days in Hartford, Connecticut, claimed
they had been "steamed" during their incarceration. On investigation, it was found that the men had been kept in a room with
no vents, no windows, and no lights, directly above a boiler.

At first, the public was well pleased with Palmer and his
agents of Justice. But in Congress, a few of Palmer's opponents

used the various sedition bill hearings as platforms from which
to criticize the attorney general. Two committees—House Rules
and House Judiciary—were told that the raids were an example
of the extensive police tactics that would be employed under the
sedition laws. The bills, one by one, disappeared. As more information about the raids came out, public opinion slowly
shifted. The liberal press denounced the Justice Department's
assault on civil liberties. The Labor Department reconsidered its
policy of supporting Palmer in the deportations. Labor officials
set about canceling more than one thousand of the sixteen hundred deportation warrants issues during the raids. Palmer, who
needed the Labor Department's approval to deport anyone,
lashed out against the Department's "tender solicitude for social
misfits," but to no avail. The ACLU published accounts of the
raids and accused the government of violating no less than four
amendments of the Bill of Rights: the Fourth, Fifth, Sixth, and
Eighth. Baldwin called for a full-scale investigation of the
Justice Department, charging that Palmer had authorized unlawful searches, used agent provocateurs, and tried to plant anti-
radical "news" articles in the press.

Across the country, the Red Scare was running out of steam.
In early 1920, five socialists elected to the New York State leg-
islature were refused admission by their fellow representatives.
By a vote of 140 to 6, the legislature expelled all five, leaving
sixty thousand citizens of the state without representation. The
ACLU protested and so did many others. The New York Bar
Association offered to represent the unseated representatives.
So did Republican Party leader Charles Evans Hughes, a distin-
guished and decidedly conservative man. "I see quite clearly,"
wrote the Reverend Father John A. Ryan, "that if the five Socialist representatives are expelled from the New York assembly
on the ground that they belong to and avow loyalty to an organization which the autocratic majority regards as 'inimical to

the best interests of the state of New York,' a bigoted majority, say the legislature of Georgia, may use the action as a precedent to keep out of that body regularly elected members who belong to the Catholic Church." It was clear that the anti-radical forces had gone too far. It was equally clear that the Russian Revolution was not as dangerous as first feared. Western Europe had not been engulfed by Communism. It seemed to some that the government was wasting time and money fighting an enemy who wasn't really there.

Palmer, who ultimately was responsible for the deportation of five hundred radicals, was never censured. But the Sedition Act that Wilson had signed in 1917 hurt Wilson's party in the November elections in 1920. The Republican Warren G. Harding won a landslide victory over the Democrat James Cox. It was a landslide fueled in part by the votes of many foreign-born citizens, angry about the Justice Department's anti-alien actions under the Espionage Act.

Eugene Debs also ran for president in 1920, again on the Socialist ticket. As in 1912, he received almost one million votes, even though his address was "care of the Atlanta Federal Prison." The Socialist Party was sorely disappointed by the count—they had hoped that, with women casting votes for the first time, Socialist candidate would do considerably better. Debs himself was little involved in politics by this point. Old and sick, he was more concerned with his fellow prisoners than with some symbolic run for office. The prison officials called him Debs a "beneficent influence" on the other men in prison. One report said that "he has caused several 'bad' men to become 'good,' and in general seems to have been able to bring about an improvement in the moral atmosphere of the institution." But Debs had not forsaken his radical roots. He told a reporter for the *New*

York World: "I am heart and soul with the Russian Revolution. Yet it is violent. I know that these great movements for human emancipation do not come without bloodshed; and although I would not kill a man in self-defense, I am in favor of shedding as much blood as is absolutely necessary in order to emancipate the people. But not one drop more."

There was a movement to get Debs released from jail on a presidential pardon. During the last weeks of the Wilson administration, Attorney General Palmer recommended that President Wilson order Debs freed. Wilson refused, saying that he would never consent "to the pardon of this man. While the flower of American youth was pouring out its blood to vindicate the cause of civilization, this man, Debs, stood behind the lines, sniping, attacking, and denouncing them." The ACLU wanted amnesty for all political prisoners. President Wilson routinely denied all requests. There were rumors of a Christmas Day pardon planned during Wilson's last year in office, but Christmas came and went without a single release.

When President Warren G. Harding took office in March 1921, he let it be known that he had not the least intention of releasing any political prisoners. The wartime Espionage Act was repealed, but Harding felt that those convicted must serve out their terms. He did meet with an ACLU delegation to discuss the matter. The delegates reminded the president that there were people serving years in jail for such crimes as criticizing the Red Cross at their own dinner table or distributing pamphlets saying that it was "un-Christian" to fight in any war. They told the president they would publicize the plight of these prisoners by picketing the White House. Harding replied that such tactics would not influence him in the slightest. When pickets were posted at the Washington Disarmament Conference, Harding did not budge from his position of no general amnesty for political prisoners. He did, however, release Eugene Debs and twenty-four other prisoners on Christmas Day, 1921. Debs was sixty-three years old, a sick man. If he died in prison, he could well become a martyr to the cause of amnesty, something Harding wanted to avoid. In New York, Governor Al Smith pardoned all prisoners held under the state's criminal anarchy law.

Far from being elated, Roger Baldwin was incensed. The ACLU's demand was one of general amnesty for all political prisoners. Such an amnesty would, in Baldwin's mind at least, be an admission of guilt on the part of the government. But in the weeks that followed the Debs release, Baldwin changed his mind, partly because someone had come to him with a new idea that just might work. Kate Richards O'Hare, a pacifist from St. Louis, contacted Baldwin about the "Children's Crusade," a program to bring the families of the political prisoners to Washington and to have the children appeal directly to the President for the release of their fathers. It was an expensive undertaking, but O'Hare scraped together enough money to bring thirty women and children to the capitol. Baldwin pledged to pay for food and housing once they got there. He had raised a special amnesty fund of five thousand dollars, getting almost half the fund from a single wealthy donor in New York. He used the money to establish an amnesty campaign headquarters in Washington, D.C., and to pay the costs of supporting the Children's Crusade.

The Crusaders raised almost five thousand dollars during their trip to Washington. They also garnered a fair amount of publicity on their trip to the capitol, and more once they set up pickets near the White House. Harding was reportedly disturbed by the sign, "Debs is Free—Why Not My Daddy?" but he refused to see the Crusaders. Mrs. O'Hare dug her heels into the sidewalk outside the White House—they would not go away. Harding relented at last. He ordered the release of all the men who promised not to "encourage, advocate, or be willfully connected with lawlessness in any form." Twelve prisoners received commutations of their sentences. Seven of them were men from the Crusader families. Mrs. O'Hare's idea had worked, but only to a point. When the men left prison, their families left Washington, and seventy-six men, almost every one of them a Wobbly, stayed behind bars for political crimes.

Baldwin, who was growing ever keener on the cause of labor, had no intention of abandoning them. He visited the prisoners held at Fort Goodman and encouraged them to apply for pardons. Most refused. An application for pardon was tantamount to an admission of guilt. Baldwin convinced several of the prisoners to allow the ACLU to petition in their behalf, and secured releases for another two dozen prisoners.

Baldwin wanted to put this issue of political prisoners behind him and to move the ACLU on to other battles. But it looked as if the some of these men would languish in jail for months, even years, under this slow process of petition, pardon, and release.

Then, on August 2, 1923, Warren Harding died while on a presidential trip to San Francisco. Baldwin had little hope for a sea change under Harding's successor, Calvin Coolidge, the taciturn former governor of Massachusetts. But less than three weeks after he took office, Coolidge requested a report on political prisoners from the Attorney General. He then set up a commission to study the situation. When the commission recommended a general amnesty, Coolidge issued it. On December 15, 1923, the last of the federal political prisoners were released from jail. But even after this general amnesty, a small number of political prisoners sat out their long sentences in state prisons across the country.

Chapter 4

We Support the First Amendment 100 Percent:
Free Speech for Labor in the 1920s

People were being lynched because of the color of their skin, women couldn't vote, the majority's religion was imposed on kids in school. Working people didn't have the right to strike. The Supreme Court had never struck down any government law on First Amendment grounds, never. The Bill of Rights existed on paper, as a marvelous invention of the people who founded the country, but no one had yet invented a way to enforce it.

—Ira Glasser

"In the case of poison gas," critic Lewis Mumford wrote in 1919, "the War Department set an excellent example by dumping large quantities of noxious compounds into the sea.... A community that had an intelligent regard for the hygiene of its mental processes would consign wartime...judicial decisions to the depths of the ocean as well." This was wishful thinking on Mumford's part. The repressive judicial decisions handed down during World War I were very much afloat. "What seems to us today," said writer Anthony Lewis, "to be the mildest sort of expression of dissent was just clamped down on viciously by the courts, even the Supreme Court." The Supreme Court had unanimously upheld the conviction of Charles T. Schenk, the general secretary of the Socialist party, who had been arrested for distributing pamphlets urging a repeal of the draft. The Supreme Court also unanimously upheld the Eugene Debs conviction. But in the case of *Abrams* v. *United States*, in which the defendants had been sentenced to twenty years for throwing anti-war pamphlets from the roof of a building in New York's garment district, Justices Holmes and Brandeis dissented. Holmes, in his moving defense of free speech, wrote: "We should be eternally vigilant against attempts to check the expression of opinions that we loathe." This dissent was the first glimmer of hope in the free speech battle but the Abrams convictions stood. "Twenty years for throwing pamphlets," said Anthony Lewis. "It was a really tough atmosphere."

It was in this tough atmosphere of the early 1920s that Roger Baldwin set about the work of creating the ACLU. He was facing an uphill climb. On two separate occasions, the *Atlantic Monthly* declined to run advertisements for the ACLU, saying that "in the past few years there has been too much civil liberty in the United States; what we need now is not more but less civil liberty."

To Baldwin fell the large and, in this climate, near-impossible task of first creating, then maintaining, the ACLU's first board of directors. As is often the case, Baldwin recruited a few famous people who would be, as he put it, "good for letterheads." But even staunch libertarians were nervous about signing on with the new organization. Harold Laski, a British citizen teaching at Harvard, felt that he, not being an American, would do more harm than good by serving on the board. Joseph Schlossberg of the Amalgamated Clothing Workers Union felt that, as a Jew, he would jeopardize the organization. Baldwin convinced both of them to join.

Baldwin also wrote letters and made recruiting phone calls to a large number of unknowns: leftists, liberals, labor leaders, socialists, and reformers who did nothing for the letterhead but who brought to the new organization a spirited mix of opinions, ideas, and personalities. There was a strong pacifist contingent from the NCLB still working with Baldwin—Crystal Eastman was on the board, and so was Jane Addams. But there were new faces as well, including Felix Frankfurter from Harvard and James Weldon Johnson of the NAACP. Fifteen of the members came from decidedly pro-labor backgrounds; Baldwin had hoped for more. But he did secure the participation of no less than five unions: the Teacher's Union of New York, the Amalgamated Textile Workers, the Telephone Operators Union, the Amalgamated Clothing Workers, and the Illinois Federation of Labor. Helen Keller served on that first board as did Elizabeth Gurley Flynn of the Workers Defense Union. Harry F. Ward, an ethics professor at Union Theological Seminary, was the chairman of the board.

From the start, Baldwin was determined to run a tight ship. He was not about to risk a mutiny like the one that had effectively ended the AUAM in 1918. To that end, he asked twenty of the board members to serve as his executive committee. With these folks he met weekly, opening each meeting with a litany of the civil liberties violations that he felt the organization should address. Typical cases he brought to the executive committee that first year included:

- In Kansas, a mob of two hundred kidnapped two organizers of the Nonpartisan League and forced the men to tar themselves. The local authorities stood by and did nothing.
- In Oregon, Lincoln Steffens was refused the right to give a lecture at a public meeting by the mayor, who felt that the meeting would be "un-American."

- In Indiana, a preacher speaking at a private meeting was kidnapped by members of the local American Legion and thrown out of town.
- In California, two realtors charged with defacing a picture of Woodrow Wilson were ordered to leave town.
- In Washington, seven IWW members were sentenced to two months in jail for selling the union's newspaper.
- In Massachusetts, a religious conscientious objector was denied citizenship.
- In Alabama, local authorities outlawed all meetings for any purpose of union coal miners.

Baldwin chose the cases carefully, then brought them to the board in such a way that they approved his every decision.

It was a grim time for civil liberties, to be sure, but the early ACLU board had a harmonious feel to it, and the tiny office staff appeared to have a downright good time. Lucille Milner, secretary, was the only woman on staff. Like Baldwin, she was a trained social worker, and like him she had done a stint as a day laborer to see how the other half lived. She proved to be a good match for Baldwin and worked for the ACLU for years, holding her own in what was, at the start, very much a man's world. When Baldwin had first met her in 1916, he had asked her whom she supported for president. "If I had the vote," she replied pointedly, "I'd cast it for Wilson." Baldwin gave as good as he got: when her first children were born—she had twins in 1922—he visited her in the hospital. "I knew you'd do a bang-up job," he said. "You always do. Efficiency first, even in the family circle."

Attorneys Albert DeSilver and Walter Nelles performed a kind of balancing act in the office. Nelles was shy and scholarly while DeSilver was outgoing, exuberant in his approach to the cases coming in. DeSilver was a wealthy man—he could afford to work for very little and often donated large sums to the young

organization. Around this staff there clustered a band of volunteer lawyers, including the flamboyant Arthur Garfield Hays, a
successful corporate attorney with a very lucrative practice.
"Life forces most men into a stodgy, dull routine," he said by way
of explaining his willingness to work for free on ACLU cases.
"Often my lawyer friends—successful men—find life drab and
uninteresting. The fight for civil liberties has given the 'salt' to
my professional work."

Baldwin did not work for free—he earned thirty-one dollars a
week. "My first wife earned her living and I earned mine, too,"
said Baldwin of those days. But Baldwin and Doty seemed to
have no trouble setting up housekeeping on their tiny incomes.
They split the bills and chores fifty-fifty. When he failed to do his
share, he paid her fifty cents an hour for the extra time she put
in. They could afford a maid (sometimes), and they were able to
throw large parties at Baldwin's rustic camp on the Hackensack
River. Baldwin invited what Doty described as "the oddest collection of people": millionaires, socialists, ex-convicts, and corporate executives. He prepared elegant meals for his guests, then
put them to work on the dishes. "Baldwin was born with a silver
spoon in his mouth," said Anthony Lewis. "He wasn't frightened
when someone called him a terrible radical. He really could cross
the lines politically, because he had friends with silver spoons on
the other side, and they knew he was really all right, if a bit ec-
centric." He was, in fact, a magnet, attracting enough members
and just enough money to keep the ACLU going. During the first
few years, expenses ran to about twenty-four thousand dollars a
year for offices, staff, and publications. Typically, about fifteen
hundred people made contributions to the Union annually, in
amounts ranging from one to one thousand dollars.

In the early 1920s, the strategy of the ACLU was one of direct
action. Baldwin favored public meetings, strategically scheduled
speeches, and publications that would influence large numbers of

people. "We had to put people on the firing line and let them get
arrested," he said, "just in order to prove that the Bill of Rights
meant what it says. That there should be no interference with
freedom of speech." Baldwin knew the ACLU could not pin its
hopes solely on the courts—the Schenk, Debs, and Abrams convictions told him this. And trying cases in court was an expensive proposition; volunteer lawyers were hard to find, particularly
outside New York City.

Baldwin kept the ACLU focused on the cause of labor at the
very time that American unions were losing both ground and
people. Organized labor lost one and a half million members in
three years, and unions were routinely stopped by local authorities in their efforts to organize. "The ACLU became connected
with the labor movement because the labor movement was
having great difficulty organizing against repressive laws," said
Anthony Lewis. "There were laws that forbade labor union organizing. State and local police forces were under the control or
effective influence of big industry, which said 'break up the
unions, break up the meetings, don't let them picket.'"

Baldwin saw this as a free speech issue. In the first annual report of the ACLU he announced that "we are not concerned to
promote any radical program, or the causes of any class. But the
circumstances of industrial conflict today force us chiefly to
champion the rights of labor to meet, organize, strike, and picket,
because labor is the class whose rights are most attacked." The
ACLU held one of its first free-speech-for-labor campaigns in
Logan County, West Virginia. This was mining country, where
80 percent of the miners lived in company-owned houses,
shopped at company-owned stores, and obeyed the laws carried
out by local officials who were themselves ruled by the mine
owners. The United Mine Workers were trying to break this
stranglehold, but their organizing efforts were crushed by the
owners time and again. In early 1920, Baldwin hired journalist

John Spivak to help the United Mine Workers in Logan County organize a free speech campaign. The companies hired gunmen to stop any union organizing and the authorities, from the local sheriff to the governor of the state, sided with the anti-union forces. Spivak, realizing the need for aggressive organizing in the face of such oppression, wrote to the ACLU office for posters and pamphlets to help in the free speech drive. Albert DeSilver wrote back, saying the material should not be too radical in nature. Spivak angrily wrote to Baldwin that the ACLU was "still under the impression that there is some semblance of legal procedure here. There is not. You can't hold a meeting here, get pinched, and then fight it out in the courts. If you try to hold a meeting...you'll never live to see the courts."

Miners who joined the union lost first their jobs, then their homes, evicted at gunpoint from their company-owned houses by company-paid thugs. Predictably, violence broke out. When a gun battle in the town of Matewan left eleven men dead, the government blamed the miners and two dozen of them were arrested for inciting violence. The ACLU handled the publicity for the trial, then publicized the mining company's civil liberties violations across the country. The trial ended in acquittal. It was a small but solid public relations victory for the ACLU; they gained in their reputation as a friend to the working man.

The ACLU continued to make good on its promise to help labor. In 1922, Baldwin sent Arthur Garfield Hays to the Pennsylvania coal fields to speak at a free speech rally. He was promptly arrested, and then, as soon as the police realized they had a prominent New York lawyer under lock and key, just as promptly released. In 1923, when four hundred members of the IWW were arrested during the California longshoreman's strike, writer Upton Sinclair and six other members held a public reading of the Constitution of the United States in San Pedro. They requested and received the mayor's permission for the reading, but Sinclair got no further than the First Amendment when police pulled him off the speaker's stand and hustled him away. Sinclair was held, incommunicado, for a day and a half. "Constitution or no Constitution, you are not going to speak in San Pedro," Police Chief Louis D. Oakes told him. Sinclair's wife tracked him down and posted bond. All the charges were dropped, and the ACLU filed unlawful arrest suits against the police, who then released the arrested Wobblies. To celebrate, Sinclair rented a large Los Angeles auditorium and held a whole series of free speech meetings. People stood in lines that wound around the building, waiting to get in.

Also in 1923, a squad made up of federal agents, city police, and company-hired detectives raided the Worker's Party headquarters in Pittsburgh. Party leaders were arrested and held without bail for ten days on trumped-up charges of a "May Day" plot. When the ACLU protested to Pennsylvania's governor, the local press accused the ACLU of supporting violence. But in this case, the ACLU was lucky. The newly-elected governor in Pennsylvania was Gifford Pinchot, a progressive with a long history of supporting social change. Pinchot was one of the country's first environmentalists. During Teddy Roosevelt's presidency Pinchot had run the Forest Service and had set aside millions of acres of forest land for conservation. He had fought and beaten the powerful utility monopolies in the West. Now he showed himself willing to take on the coal industry. He intervened on labor's behalf in the wage disputes and appointed a commission to study the police forces that were being used to keep labor down. The commission's study was an indictment of the coal industry and the public officials that served it, listing over one hundred cases of illegal violence and repression perpetrated by public officials on the union in the year 1922. The report was widely circulated, and public opinion about labor unions slowly began to change. When the Kansas Industrial

Court ruled that townspeople in Emporia, Kansas, could not display a placard reading "WE ARE FOR THE STRIKING RAILROAD MEN 100 PERCENT," William Allen White, editor of the Emporia *Gazette*, immediately put one up in his office window. But White revised the numbers on the sign: his read that he was for the strikers "49 percent." White had won a Pulitzer Prize that year for a pro–free speech editorial. With his sign he was showing support, not for labor, but for the First Amendment. "If the strike lasts until tomorrow we shall change the percent to 50, and move it up a little every day. As a matter of fact, the *Gazette* does not believe that anyone—not even the *Gazette*—is 100 percent right," he wrote. "This is not a question of whether the men are right or wrong, but a question of the right of an American citizen to say what he pleases about the strike. And if 49 percent sympathy is permissible, in the next fifty days we shall see where violation of the law begins." As it turned out, the Industrial Court ruled that the violation began at 50 percent and that the *Gazette* sign must come down. When White refused, he was arrested. When the charges were dropped, White demanded a trial, but the court would not give him one. As White said, "It did not dare to."

In 1924, one critical labor case involved Roger Baldwin himself. When eight thousand silk workers went out on strike in Paterson, New Jersey, the mill owners got no fewer than fifteen injunctions making it illegal for strikers to picket. "The police just closed all strike halls and said 'no more meetings,'" said Roger Baldwin. "I went over to Paterson from New York because the strike leaders asked me to come. They said, 'What are you going to do about opening up these halls?' And I decided we'd have a public meeting on the city hall steps. We'll get a lot of American flags and we'll have a parade down to the city hall. We'll show them that this is the Bill of Rights that we're defending."

And Baldwin went, leading thirty protesters with flags to city hall. "And as soon as we got to the city hall and started making speeches in favor of the Bill of Rights, the police cracked our heads and broke us up." A number of demonstrators were arrested, but not Roger Baldwin himself. "I had organized the affair and I was not arrested," he said. "I was determined I would be. I went down to police headquarters and insisted on being arrested." Baldwin, as usual, got what he wanted: he was charged with "rout, riot, and unlawful assembly," and given a six-month sentence. He made bail and appealed. "I had a case in the New Jersey court, and finally got acquitted by unanimous opinion of the Supreme Court of New Jersey," he recalled. "I showed them I *was* doing the right thing defending the Bill of Rights on the city hall steps."

Albert DeSilver called A. Mitchell Palmer's immediate successor, Harry M. Daugherty, "the nice fat man with a big cigar in his face," adding that "instead of getting excited as Palmer used to do, he grins when somebody talks about revolution and says, well he thinks it probably best 'not to agitate the agitator' too much." But Daugherty was not really all that nice. He kept the "radical" surveillance division at the Justice Department intact. William J. Burns, owner of a large and profitable private detective agency, was in charge. Burns saw danger everywhere, particularly in the ACLU. He had agents keep close tabs on Baldwin and his staff. They tracked their public activities, tapped their phones, and got hold of membership and donor lists. At a congressional hearing Burns denounced the ACLU as a communist front, saying that communism had "sprung up everywhere, as evidenced by this American Civil Liberties Union of New York. Wherever we seek to suppress these radicals, a civil liberties union promptly gets busy." But Burns had absolutely no proof of any treasonous plots going on; his surveillance and raids on

Communist Party meetings had yielded nothing. The *New York World* editorialized that Burns was "the only man in the United States who can still see that famous Red revolution coming." The FBI, said the ACLU in one of its reports, had become "a secret police system of a political character."

In 1924, Burns was gone, one of the first Justice Department officials to lose his job when President Coolidge made Harlan Fiske Stone his attorney general. Stone, a law professor from Columbia and a widely-respected jurist, reorganized the Bureau of Investigation. "There is always the possibility that a secret police system may become a menace to a free government," Stone said. In May, he ordered the Bureau to limit itself to the investigation of violations of federal statutes. He did keep J. Edgar Hoover on as the "acting" head of the Bureau, a move which initially angered the ACLU. But Hoover's public proclamations were conciliatory, even contrite. He told a congressional committee investigating the Justice Department that "instructions have been sent to officers in the field to limit their investigations in the field to violation of statutes," and he promised to "eliminate from the forces such deadwood as has been in the [FBI]." In a face-to-face meeting, Hoover assured Baldwin that he had been an "unwilling" participant in the Palmer raids. Baldwin, ever the optimist, pronounced him a "decent enough fellow."

Behind the scenes, Hoover complained to Stone in a long and bitter memorandum about the ACLU and its charges against the FBI. He defended his actions during the Palmer raids, and denied that the Bureau had ever used wiretapping or other surveillance devices against the ACLU. Nevertheless, Hoover told Stone, the Bureau would comply with all new policies; the days of the secret police were over. At the very same time, however, Hoover's agents were assembling hundreds of pages of evidence against ACLU activities in California. The agents reported on legal plans, infiltrated the ACLU's committees, and at least once dissuaded a California judge from participating in an ACLU forum. Agents routinely worked with local police "red squads" involved in radical surveillance. In 1927 and 1928, Hoover ordered investigations of the New York office of the ACLU. All this activity was carried on in secrecy; to Baldwin, to Attorney General Stone, and, in fact, to the world, it appeared that J. Edgar Hoover was playing by the rules.

"American questions should be settled in America by Americans." This was an oft-heard slogan in the Ku Klux Klan in its resurgence. One million members strong in 1921, the Klan spread a gospel of "practical patriotism" not just in the South but in every part of the country. Only "native-born, white American citizens, who believe in the tenets of Christian religion," were truly American. The Klan believed that Negroes, Jews, Catholics, and immigrants should be kept out of power, and, ideally, out of the country. Victims of the Klan's notorious night riders were subjected to intimidation, beating, kidnapping, and worse; between 1920 and 1925 six murders were attributed to the Klan. It was a record that did not impress Roger Baldwin. "We're against discrimination against any minority in the United States," he once said. "If that discrimination is expressed in denial of any of the rights guaranteed by the Constitution we of course would act."

For most of the decade, the Justice Department showed surprisingly little interest in the Klan's activities. It was the ACLU that tracked the cases, kept the records, and publicized the KKK's repeated civil liberties violations. But at the same time the ACLU condemned the KKK, it also represented them. "We had some complaints about the denial of the Klan's right to parade in their nightgowns and pillowcases, and their right to burn fiery crosses on private property," said Baldwin. "We decided that we had to defend their rights.... The Imperial Wizard responded by thanking us for our generous expressions of true Americanism, and telling us that they would be glad to accept our services." When the NAACP tried to stop the Klan from sending its hate message through the U.S. mail, the ACLU argued for the KKK. And even though the NAACP's James Weldon Johnson sat on Baldwin's board, the ACLU also stepped in when the NAACP attempted to stop the exhibition of the racist film, *Birth of a Nation*. This equal opportunity advocacy did not stop with the Klan. When city officials in Cleveland and Toledo banned Henry Ford's viciously anti-Semitic newspaper, the *Dearborn Independent*, the ACLU came out for Ford. "Every view, no matter how ignorant or harmful we may regard it, had a legal and moral right to be heard," was the ACLU's position. Every view? Even one that accused the Jews of running roughshod over the press, American politics, banking, and baseball? "The rowdyism that has afflicted baseball," said a writer in Ford's *Independent*, "is all of Jewish origin." They have a right to say it, said Baldwin. He was determined, it seemed, to support free speech and to stir up controversy.

Chapter 5

The Monkey Trial:
The ACLU Goes to Tennessee

*The ACLU will be battling about the issues raised in the
Scopes trial so long as there is a United States of America.*
                                        —Nat Hentoff

Roger Baldwin was not overly concerned about the theory of
evolution. Perhaps a man with a solid Mayflower pedigree
wouldn't be bothered by the notion of a few monkeys swinging
from the upper branches of the family tree. But Baldwin was
bothered when teachers were told they couldn't discuss evolution in their classrooms. The ACLU studied the problem in
depth, and in 1924 released the results of a study on restrictive
laws in schools and colleges. In that year there were more restrictive teaching laws on the books than at any other time in
America's history. These were laws that required Bible reading
and religious study in public school, that barred pacifists from
being teachers, and that forbade the teaching of evolution and
other "radical" notions.

Evolution had not always been considered a radical idea in this
country. True, Darwin had pulled the carpet out from under the
feet of Biblical creation in 1857 by stating that Adam had not
been created on the sixth day, but had evolved, over time, from
something like a monkey. Shocking stuff. But a sort of truce came

about, partly because Darwin himself wrote that the evolution and Genesis were not entirely disparate. "There is grandeur in this view of life," he wrote, "having been originally breathed by the Creator into a few forms or into one; and that . . . from so simple a beginning endless forms most beautiful and most wonderful have been and are being evolved."

In the United States, the theory of evolution was taught in school and mentioned in textbooks as early as 1895. But around 1910, evolution became a "dangerous" idea, somehow "un-American." Darwin, along with short skirts and demon rum, was undermining American values. The Anti-Evolution League of America launched a nation-wide "Bible-Christ-and-Constitution Campaign against Evolution in Tax-Supported Schools." The Annual Convention of Southern Baptists in 1923 said that science must acknowledge the Bible as its principal authority—the Virgin Birth, the physical Resurrection, and the Second Coming must be treated as fact. In 1924, the Arkansas Baptist Convention ruled that no Baptist institution could employ anyone, not even a janitor, who believed in evolution. Fundamentalists across the South insisted that the schools must teach what the Bible says, and the Bible says nothing about Adam descending from an ape.

Fervor in the churches spilled over into government. In 1925, John Washington Butler, a farmer and second-term Tennessee state legislator, authored a bill that would prohibit the teaching of evolution in all universities, normal schools (teachers' training schools), and public schools in the state. There was no real opposition to the bill that he submitted to legislature. There was no real support either, until a few Baptist ministers, hoping to attract attention and converts, took it on as a cause. This anti-evolution bill, they claimed, was a necessary defense against modernism. It quickly became a popular cause in the state and with the Baptist support, Butler's bill sailed through the house, seventy-one to five, and the senate, twenty-four to six. "I had to vote for it," said one legislator. "It had been put up to my constituents that if I voted against the bill I would be voting against the Bible." On March 21, 1925, Governor Austin Peay signed H.B. 185 of the Public Acts of Tennessee of 1925 into law, but few people took it seriously. Governor Peay himself said that "nobody believes that it is going to be an active statute." In a way, he was right. The law, which would stay on the Tennessee books for almost a half century, was enforced exactly once, in the case of *John Thomas Scopes* v. *The State of Tennessee.*

It was the ever-vigilant Lucille Milner who first spotted the three column-inch news item in the *Chattanooga Times*: Tennessee had itself a new anti-evolution law. Milner took the news straight to Baldwin, who went straight to the press. "We sent a release to the newspapers in Tennessee saying 'anybody who wants to violate that law will get our help. And we got a fellow who volunteered, Mr. Scopes."

John Thomas Scopes, a Tennessee-born, Illinois-trained teacher at the Rhea County High School of Dayton, did not exactly volunteer. He was talked into it by Dayton's George Rappalyea, a liberal town booster who believed the publicity would do the small town some good. He also believed that Scopes was the right teacher to challenge the anti-evolution law. Scopes was self-effacing, affable, popular. It was not unusual to see him downtown of an evening, talking with the young men from the football team. The superintendent had cautioned Scopes about "buddying" around with the boys. Scopes showed his backbone by replying, "If a teacher can't mix up with folks, I'm through with teaching." He continued to mix, joining young men on the street corner, or at the soda fountain table in F. E. Robinson's drugstore, which is exactly where Rappalyea and a few other townsfolk cornered him and convinced him to challenge the new law with help from the ACLU.

"I knew there would be a certain amount of publicity," Scopes said later, "and that a great portion of our society would believe I had some kind of horns. At the same time, I knew that sooner or later someone would have to take a stand against the stifling of freedom that the Butler Act represented." Scopes took his stand and Rappalyea wired Baldwin. Baldwin wired back: WE WILL COOPERATE SCOPES CASE WITH FINANCIAL HELP, LEGAL ADVICE, AND PUBLICITY." Scopes was arrested on May 7, 1925, and charged with teaching the theory of evolution. His bond was fixed at one thousand dollars and the trial was set for the coming summer. "I don't think we ever dreamed," said Baldwin, "that it would attract the international attention that it did. From a point of view of publicity, it was the most famous case we ever had."

Much of the case's fame stemmed from the trial's two great protagonists. For the prosecution, there was William Jennings Bryan, the most famous religious fundamentalist in America. Bryan's public career spanned four decades. He had been a three-time presidential candidate on the Democratic ticket and he had served as secretary of state under Wilson. Bryan was the largest draw on the Chatauqua lecture circuit, and had been for more than thirty years. He was slightly larger than life, a massive man, who in one breakfast could eat six eggs with ham, pancakes drowned in butter, many plates of hash browns, a large melon, and a brace of quail.

For the defense, there was Clarence Darrow of Chicago, who was, in Baldwin's words, "an extraordinarily able lawyer." Folksy, canny, and theatrical, Darrow had been practicing law full-tilt since he had first been admitted to the Ohio Bar in 1878. He had been counsel for the city of Chicago and had then turned to labor law, representing Eugene Debs in the Pullman Strike case of 1894. He next turned to criminal law, successfully defending Big Bill Haywood against his Idaho murder charge in 1907. "I speak for the poor, the weak, the weary," he told the jury in that case, "for that long line of men who, in darkness and despair, have borne the labors of the human race." In 1924 he took on the case of two young men from well-to-do families, Nathan Leopold and Richard Loeb, saving them from execution after they had been convicted of a shockingly cold-blooded murder. In fact, of the more than fifty murder cases Darrow had taken on, only one had ended in execution.

Darrow volunteered for the defense, as did three other lawyers: Dudley Field Malone and Arthur Garfield Hays of New York, and John Randolph Neal of Tennessee. These three were delighted to be working with the famous Clarence Darrow, but not everyone shared their enthusiasm. In New York, at the ACLU office, Walter Nelles, who handled much of the detail work on the Scopes case, maneuvered behind the scenes to dump both Darrow and Malone—Malone because he was a high-living, high society divorce lawyer, Darrow because he was too much the showman, and too much identified with radicals. But the Chicago lawyer had an influential champion outside the ACLU—Scopes himself. At a June defense team meeting in New York, Scopes insisted Darrow be on the team, and Nelles acquiesced. It would be Darrow, Malone, Hays, and Neal for the defense.

Bryan took the case at the behest of the World's Christian Fundamentals Association, and the town attorneys prosecuting Scopes welcomed the participation of such a famous man. But the Bryan who came to Dayton was an old man, a lawyer who had not practiced law for thirty-five years. He was troubled by heart disease, and troubled by the Butler law itself, which he found vague and poorly written. But he kept his unhappiness to himself and plunged into the carnival atmosphere that prevailed in the town that summer. The prosecution was something of a family affair: it included Bryan's son, William; Ben MacKenzie and his son, Gordon; and the Hicks brothers, Sue and Herbert. All told, there were a dozen lawyers involved in the case, but only Darrow and Bryan truly held the nation's attention. "With these two powerful figures clashing," said Anthony Lewis, "the Scopes trial pitted what could be called modern America against what H. L. Mencken called the 'Bible Belt.'" In a way, it was a battle destined to take place. Darrow was an avowed agnostic, Bryan a religious leader. Darrow lived in the seamy, political world of Chicago; Bryan, who lived in a Florida mansion, touted himself as a man of the countryside. Both were Democrats, but Darrow came from the end of the party built by labor, Bryan from the faction that believed in agrarian control. Bryan was arguably the most famous public speaker of the day. Darrow, known for his silver-tongued oratory, was ready to rob Bryan of the title.

H. L. Mencken of the *Baltimore Sun* was only one of the swarm of reporters that descended on Dayton in early July to cover the pre-trial hoopla. According to the Associated Press there were more than one hundred newspapers represented at the trial; the average daily press file was 165,000 words. It was the first trial ever to be broadcast live over the radio. "My gavel," boasted Judge John Raulston, "will be heard around the world."

The press made much of the carnival atmosphere surrounding the trial. "Dayton has its circus, the nation its summer enter-tainment, while the question of the origin of man is lowered to the level of horse play," wrote one reporter. Mencken made much of the backwoods townsfolk, calling them "hillbillies" and "peasants." But Mencken also poked fun at the ACLU and at the high horse of civil liberties on which it rode. "We are asked to believe that some mysterious and vastly important principle is at stake at Dayton," he wrote. "No principle is at stake in Dayton, save the principle that school teachers, like plumbers, should stick to the job that is set before them, and not go roving about the house, breaking windows, raiding the cellar, and demoralizing the children."

"The case was an immense public event," said the ACLU's Burt Neuborne. "It riveted public attention on the issue, and it brought the ACLU to the attention of millions of Americans who had never heard of the organization." *The New York Times*, in an editorial, said that the case "gives scientific men a better opportunity than they ever had to bring their teaching home to millions." The scientists "will have a larger and more alert popular audience than they have ever known." The audience was large, and it was alert, but not necessarily to the science of the case. By early July, it was possible to buy soda pop, Bibles, and monkey dolls on every street corner in town. Robinson's Drugstore sold a "Monkey Fizz"; store windows were stacked with little cotton apes, monkey back-scratchers, and monkey watch fobs. You could have your picture taken with a live chimpanzee or be baptized at the Holy Roller Revival being held on nearby Shin Bone Ridge. There was soapbox preaching and organ-grinding, and signs reading "Come to Jesus" and "Read Your Bible" were plastered all over town—even in the courtroom itself. "Ringling Brothers or Barnum & Bailey would have been hard pressed to produce more acts and sideshows and freaks than Dayton had," said Scopes.

The lawyers were part of the show. A huge crowd turned out to welcome Bryan and followed him as he strolled the streets, eating radishes, waving a palm fan, and predicting that the case would result in a great religious revival. "New York City's notion of the greatest show on earth is the *Follies* with Mr. Will Rogers," wrote one reporter. "At Dayton the greatest intellectual treat is the summoning of the scientists to testify as to all theories of creation. On this showing which is the moron city?"

~

The prosecution planned a simple case: John Scopes was guilty of violating a Tennessee law. The defense strategy was more complicated: according to Hays, the defense team wished to show that the law was unconstitutional because it made the Bible the test of truth—in Darrow's words, "the law makes the Bible the yardstick." Furthermore, the law was vague and unenforceable. No two persons understand the Bible in exactly the same way. Finally, the law was, in the light of contemporary science, unreasonable. To prove this last point, the defense assembled an impressive slate of expert witnesses—professors of geology, zoology, and education brought in from Harvard, the University of Chicago, and the University of Missouri. The state geologist of Tennessee was prepared to testify for the defense. Hays later said that "the anti-evolution case in Tennessee gave me something better than a college education on questions of evolution and the Bible."

Before the trial began, the ACLU sought to have the case moved to federal court, a venue presumably more appropriate to a case involving First Amendment issues of free speech and separation of church and state. But the federal court said no. On July 10, 1925, the trial began in Dayton. Opening day was a tedious disappointment to the large crowd in the courtroom. The defense moved to quash the indictment, saying that the charge was "vague" and the law unconstitutional. The state argued, and Judge Raulston agreed, that the charge was sufficiently specific, and that the Tennessee state legislature was within its rights in passing the act. Then the lawyers squabbled over the admissibility of scientific evidence. Onlookers and reporters sweated, dozed, and shared bottles of soda pop. Jurors used the fans they had received from a toothpaste company, emblazoned with the slogan "Do Your Gums Bleed?" to keep themselves cool.

Then, finally, the trial began in earnest. "When on the fourth day after the opening of the famous trial Clarence Darrow arose with the characteristic hitch of his shoulders and began his first electrical speech," wrote one reporter, "a tremor ran through the assembled army of newspapermen as they awoke with a start from the spell which Dayton had cast on them." Darrow's opening statement was a classic: "If today you can take a thing like evolution and make it a crime to teach it . . . after a while it is the setting of man against man, and creed against creed, until with flying banners and beating drums we are marching backward to the glorious age of the sixteenth century, when bigots lighted faggots to burn the men who dared bring any intelligence and enlightenment and culture to the human mind."

Bryan's first speech began with equal passion. "The Christian believes that man came from above; but the evolutionist believes he must have come from below!" He railed against biology textbooks that gave more space on the page to animals than to humans. But although Bryan started strong, he soon ran out of steam. It was, as one reporter wrote "a plea as uncorrupted as possible by any knowledge." Time and again Malone rose to break the rhythm of his speech, time and again Bryan faltered. But no matter; Judge Raulston ruled as Bryan had asked: no scientist would be allowed to testify in Dayton.

It was a victory for the prosecution, a disappointment to the crowd, and a catastrophe for the defense plan. During the weekend recess, Darrow came up with another: he would put the Bible itself on trial. In a display of unparalleled courtroom hubris, he called Bryan to the stand as an expert on fundamentalism. The state objected; Judge Raulston, who would not allow a scientific expert take the stand, ruled that a biblical expert could. Bryan was one very unhappy witness, and for good reason. Darrow's attack was brutally effective. Under cross-examination, Bryan duly maintained that the Bible was, without exception, literally true. Darrow's questions came on relentlessly:

"Do you believe that Jonah remained three days in the whale's belly?"

"The Bible says that every living creature not on Noah's ark was drowned...does that mean the fishes drowned?"

"The sun stood still for Joshua...does that mean that the sun was moving around the earth before that?"

Bryan fell into every trap, and ended up making retorts such as, "I do not think about things I don't think about," and left the stand devastated. "For a moment," wrote Joseph Krutch, "one was almost sorry for the great leader brought so low."

The Scopes trial has been called the ACLU's "first great triumph," but the result of the trial was no triumph. The trial lasted eight days and the jury took just nine minutes to reach a verdict: Scopes was guilty as charged. Judge Raulston delivered the sentence: Scopes was fined one hundred dollars.

The ACLU planned an immediate appeal, and Baldwin looked forward to taking the matter all the way to the Supreme Court. But there was a problem. "We in the ACLU were urged from several influential sources to engage a different type of counsel," he said. "Darrow...might be first-rate for such a performance as that required with Bryan as the chief prosecutor, but the Supreme Court of Tennessee was no place for a contest of wits and philosophies." Once again Scopes intervened; he wanted Darrow to stay on, and Darrow himself wanted very much to stay on. He told Baldwin that "justice depends upon kind what kind of a lawyer you have—you'd better hire me." There was no possibility of a Darrow-Bryan rematch; William Jennings Bryan died of heart failure only nine days after the trial ended. And in the end, the post-trial infighting was moot. On first appeal, the state supreme court reversed the Scopes decision on a technicality. Judge Raulston had imposed a fine of one hundred dollars, when state law required that any fine over fifty dollars was to be imposed by the jury, not the judge. Thomas Scopes never had his day before the Supreme Court.

To some, the Monkey Trial had its silver lining. "The statute," said Ira Glasser, "was never enforced again. And basically the anti-evolution law became the laughingstock of the country." Over the next two years, laws prohibiting the teaching of evolution were defeated in twenty-two states. But the Monkey Trial had a chilling effect as well. The teaching of evolution declined precipitously after 1925. Most science teachers simply ignored the theory and many biology texts published between 1930 and 1960 did not use the words "evolution" or "Darwin." What's more, the Tennessee law stayed on the books. When a bill calling for repeal was proposed in 1961, it was promptly defeated. Writing on Scopes and evolution in *The New York Times* in 1971, W. Dykemand and J. Stokely announced that "the jury is still out."

"It seems quite amazing," said Anthony Lewis, "that the Scopes trial should still have any relevance to us today. But there are still forces in this country very vigorously trying to insist on the teaching of what they call creationism, and forbidding the teaching of the theory of evolution. Just going on right now. So it's not by any means a dead issue."

The Monkey Trial's most lasting effect could be seen in the ACLU itself. In the years and decades that followed, the ACLU would go by its own book: there must be absolute separation of church and state. That word "absolute," at times, has turned the ACLU into the Grinch who stole Christmas. Public resources must never go to sectarian causes—no Nativity scenes on the lawn at city hall, please. To some it seems ludicrous, but writer

Molly Ivins defends even these tactics by citing an 1803 letter written by James Madison: "This is what he said. 'The purpose of separation of church and state is to keep forever from these shores the ceaseless strife that has soaked the soil of Europe with blood for centuries.' Still does. The soil of Bosnia soaked with blood.... That principle is so important that it's worth being a pain in the ass about. And that's what the ACLU is."

"Full of uplift and confidence." Roger Baldwin shortly after finishing Harvard. (*Mudd Library, Princeton University*)

An IWW rally in Union Square, New York, 1908. *(National Archives)*

Elizabeth Gurley Flynn (center) with members of the Butte Miners Union in Montana in 1909. Flynn was an IWW activist, a free speech advocate, and a founding member of the ACLU. *(Taminent Institute Library, New York University)*

Pacifists in the United States were a vocal group. These are petitions presented to Congress by the American Women for Strict Neutrality, 1916. *(Library of Congress)*

An anti-war rally held in New York, August, 1914. *(Library of Congress)*

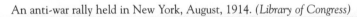

Women attending one of the hundreds of pacifist rallies held in the United States before the country entered the war. (*Library of Congress*)

Secretary of War Newton Baker draws numbers for the second draft, June 1918. (*National Archives*)

Recruits being sworn into the U.S. military at a New York City recruiting station, 1918. (*National Archives*)

Patriotic fever—Americans marching in a loyalty parade. (*Library of Congress*)

The consequences of free speech. Above: Upton Sinclair reads the Bill of Rights in San Pedro, California, 1923; below: Upton Sinclair arrested in San Pedro, 1923. (*The ACLU of Southern California*)

Crystal Eastman of the AUAM with Amos Pinchot. (*Library of Congress*)

Eugene V. Debs, Socialist Party leader and perennial presidential candidate.
(*The ACLU of Southern California*)

Emma Goldman, anarchist, deportee, and Roger Baldwin's mentor.
(*National Archives*)

Norman Thomas, Socialist and founding ACLU member. *(Library of Congress)*

Madeline Doty, international peace activist and Baldwin's first wife, 1913.
(*Sophia Smith Collection, Smith College*)

Roger Baldwin, 1919. *(Sophia Smith Collection, Smith College)*

Attorney General A. Mitchell Palmer, 1920. A Quaker from Pennsylvania, Palmer was responsible for the illegal arrest of hundreds of Americans during the infamous raids that bear his name. (*Library of Congress*)

J. Edgar Hoover in his Justice Department Office. After 1924, he ran the Bureau of Investigation as a private police force, secretly keeping tabs on ACLU members and hundreds of thousands of Americans suspected of radical behavior. (*National Archives*)

One of the two great protangonists in the "Monkey Trial," Clarence Darrow. (*Library of Congress*)

The other great protagonist in the "Monkey Trial," William Jennings Bryan. (*Tennessee State Library and Archives*)

John Scopes, 1925. *(Library of Congress)*

Rhea County Central High School football team, 1924. Coach John Scopes sits in the upper left-hand corner. *(Tennessee State Library and Archives)*

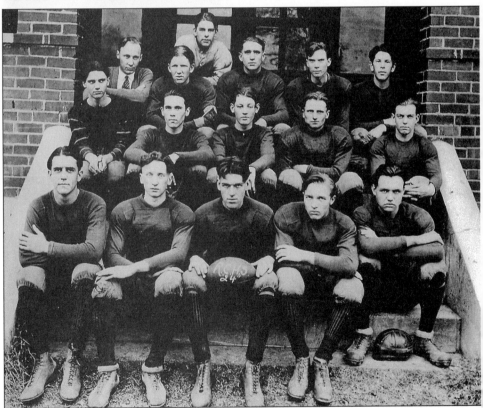

Courtroom and jury shortly before deliberation begins in the Scopes case, 1925. *(Tennessee State Library and Archives)*

Citizens on the streets of Dayton, Tennessee. *(Tennessee State Library and Archives)*

Girls with their monkey dolls pose for the press in Dayton. (*Tennessee State Library and Archives*)

"The Scopes Case." (*The National Archives*)

John Scopes shakes hand with Clarence Darrow. (*Tennessee State Library and Archives*)

Worker's Alliance March in New York, 1934. Labor in the 1930s continued to press for the right to organize. *(National Archives)*

"I am the law in Jersey City." No friend to the worker, the dapper Mayor Frank Hague (here with his wife) routinely "outlawed" labor activity in Jersey City. (*Library of Congress*)

Labor strife. Above: police attack labor demonstrators in Los Angeles in the 1930s; below: wounded demonstrators on the sidewalk. *(The ACLU of Southern California)*

The Workers Alliance: a 1930s march that shows the coming together of Communism, Socialism, and labor. *(Library of Congress)*

Chapter 6

The Grail of Free Speech:
The Victories of the 1930s

Throughout my years as president of the ACLU, almost fifteen years, there were dozens of occasions when on talk shows people would say, "Well, what can you expect of the ACLU, the founder of the ACLU was a communist." And I would explain that Roger Baldwin wasn't a communist, that he had a brief flirtation with the ideas of communism.

—*Norman Dorsen*

Roger Baldwin had stood to one side during much of the Scopes trial, not because he feared the spotlight, but because he was knee-deep in several labor disputes. He was a busy man. "I was not then," he recalled, "nor have I been since, confined wholly to my main job." An understatement. In the twenties and thirties Baldwin skated through liberal America's political landscape. He was an influential player in the National Urban League, the Fellowship of Reconciliation, the International Committee for Political Prisoners, the League Against Imperialism, the League for Peace and Democracy, and the Friends of the Soviet Union. That many of these groups had strong ties to communism, both the American and Russian varieties, was entirely in keeping with his "main job." Baldwin was, after all, the director of an organization that championed free speech for labor. "Most of the controversial speech that was going on in the country went on around the labor movement," said Burt Neuborne of the ACLU. "So we tended to represent a very large number of labor organizers during the thirties. And large numbers of the labor organizers during the thirties were so-cialists or communists."

Baldwin was no stranger to the ideals of communism. Like many liberal Americans, he nurtured dreams of an idealized soci-ety, using tools like the hammer and sickle. In the 1920s, he, along with a few friends in the IWW, joined the board of the Kuzbas Industrial Colony, an experiment in cooperative living in the Soviet Union. The board recruited American volunteers to live and work in a collective community in the Urals; they raised half a million dollars for the community and sent them farm machinery and supplies. Kuzbas proved as short-lived as it was idealistic—the experiment fell flat within months. One return-ing colonist, disgruntled by the whole experience, charged Bald-win and the rest of the Kuzbas board with second degree larceny in the handling of colony funds. The board was indicted, but Arthur Garfield Hays quickly got the charges dropped.

Undaunted, Baldwin tried again, this time with the Recon-struction Farm in southern Russia. He helped raise money in America to send farm machinery and supplies to the farm. It did well, but as a whole this experiment, too, failed when the Soviet government refused to make good on bonds that had been sold to finance the venture.

Still Baldwin did not give up on the Russians. In 1927, he spent three months in the Soviet Union, investigating the polit-ical prisoner situation for the International Committee on Polit-ical Prisoners and researching a book on civil liberty under the Soviet regime. It was a sort of sentimental journey for him. He visited the region of the Reconstruction Farm and thought that the place "looked like Kansas: miles of wheat and tons of machines." He took a room in the home of the late anarchist Peter Kropotkin. "I rejoiced," he wrote, "to live in the same quarters my anarchist teacher had occupied." But his prison investigation was not nearly so pleasant. The political prisoners he saw were held under tight control and harsh conditions. There were many he did not see. The Soviets would not permit him access to the notorious Lubianka prison—his guides told him it was an "abnormal" time there. "It was evident," he later wrote, "that the government had locked up, after only the most superficial trials or none at all, persons against whom charges of obstruction had been brought. The stories I heard astonished me, because they concerned such apparently insubstantial crimes."

Baldwin left Russia in an ambivalent frame of mind. He knew dissent was not tolerated in the Soviet Union, but he was loathe to criticize the "great experiment." His book *Liberty Under the Soviets*, published in 1928, was an apologia for the Communists. "Repressions in western democracies are violations of professed constitutional liberties, and I condemn them as such. Repressions in Soviet Russia are weapons of struggle in a transition period to socialism." This kind of thinking was a double standard that irritated many Americans. "Why is it," asked Walter Lippmann about Communist supporters, "that they are indignant when Mr. Burleson suppresses a newspaper and complacent when Lenin does?"

"There's no question," said William Donohue, a sociologist with the Catholic League for Religious and Civil Rights and a longtime critic of the ACLU, "that throughout the 1920s and 1930s Roger Baldwin was, as he called himself, a fellow traveler in communist circles. He was clearly very much aligned with the communists in many things." In fact, Baldwin was never a Communist Party member, but his keen interest in the Party reflected a pattern that defined the liberalism of the time. "During the thirties it became acceptable, even fashionable, for liberals to work with and cooperate with communists for common goals," said historian Mary McAuliffe. Indeed, with Hitler and Nazism on the rise in Germany and the Great Depression taking hold in America, communism looked good to many people. "When you're young and just coming into the world, you see things that upset you—people in the streets, poverty everywhere," said actress Betty Garrett, who joined the American Communist Party in the 1930s. "The Communist Party seemed to be the only organization trying to do something about these things. They held parades in New York City, demanding food and housing for the poor. Nobody else was doing that."

Baldwin was not the only ACLU official excited by communism. Harry Ward chaired both the ACLU and the prominent United Front organization, the American League for Peace and Democracy. But the ACLU had its share of anti-communists as well. Norman Thomas, leader of the crumbling American Socialist Party, viewed the Communist Party as competition. Board member John Haynes Holmes even suggested to Baldwin that they keep communists off the board of the ACLU. Holmes called the communists "a group of savages, who, like their Nazi competitors, make war upon all members of the human race excepting themselves." Perhaps the most staunch of the anti-communists at the Union was General Counsel Morris Ernst. A fierce supporter of Franklin Roosevelt, Ernst had worked with Baldwin since the ACLU's founding, and had become more influential as the years went on. Albert DeSilver had been killed in a freak train accident in 1924; Walter Nelles was still with the Union, but would eventually leave to take on a teaching position elsewhere. Baldwin was in charge, but Ernst, along with Arthur Garfield Hays, set the legal course for the organization.

By the early thirties, Baldwin ran both hot and cold when it came to the Communist Party. In an author's note to later editions of *Liberty under the Soviets* he added a "word of caution" about the growing control that the Soviet government was exerting over trade unions, religion, and the peasant cooperatives. He conceded that repression—that "necessary weapon"—was being overused, and alluded to the imprisonments and summary executions being carried out by the Communists in Russia. But the economic gains of Communism left him with "the underlying sympathy and hope" he had felt in 1928. "In other words," he wrote, "while I have not changed my view of Russia, the facts have changed their emphasis."

Baldwin's criticism of some international Soviet policies cost him the chairmanship of a United Front organization, the League Against Imperialism. When he tried to visit Russia in 1934, his support of Trotsky's sanctuary in Mexico cost him his visa. Still, that same year, he wrote an article that would later prove embarrassing: "When power of the working class is once achieved, I am for maintaining it by any means whatever. Dictatorship is the obvious means in a world of enemies...Communism is the goal," he wrote, not sounding much like a civil libertarian. But when communists broke up a mass Socialist Party meeting in Madison Square Garden, Baldwin instinctively recoiled. The rally, called to protest Nazi aggression in Europe, was to have signaled leftist solidarity against the fascists. Instead, it demonstrated that discord on the left had fallen to the level of fisticuffs. One writer covering the rally was seriously hurt in the brawl. "Such tactics," said Baldwin, "make cooperation with communists ineffective."

Communists, the Nazi Party in America, and the Klan were all guided by the simple rule, "free speech for us and nobody else—and not much for us either." Nevertheless, when their free speech rights were being trampled, it was the ACLU's practice to defend them. It was a position that Baldwin had to defend over and over again during the twenties and thirties. In *Shall We Defend Free Speech for Nazis in America?*, Baldwin wrote "to those of you who advocate suppressing propaganda they hate, we ask—where do you draw the line?" As the decade advanced, the ACLU found support for this position coming from an unexpected source—the Supreme Court. In several key decisions, the Court discarded the limited definition of free speech that dominated the World War I era. In one case the Court pronounced "freedom of speech and the press...are among the fundamental rights and 'liberties' protected by the due process clause of the Fourteenth Amendment." In a second they held that "no danger can be deemed clear and present, unless the incidence of the evil apprehended is so imminent that it may befall before there is opportunity for full discussion." And full discussion was what the ACLU was after: In one year, they were defending the right of the Ku Klux Klan to hold meetings in Catholic-dominated Boston, the right of Catholics to hold teaching jobs in Akron's KKK-dominated school system, and the right of Rhode Island communists to show movies against the combined opposition of the KKK and the Catholic Church. And it was not just political speech that they were protecting. Although the ACLU had steered clear when Boston banned sixty-five books in a public decency campaign in 1926, they jumped in when the ban was extended to speech. It was one thing to have a sex education pamphlet banned, but another to stand by when Boston would not permit Margaret Sanger to speak.

The ACLU had joined the anti-censorship campaign. After Boston, Arthur Hays and Morris Ernst engineered a virtual crusade against censorship that, like Scopes, presented the ACLU as the champion of enlightenment and common sense. They attacked censorship at the movies and defended Mary Dennett's sex education books for young people. In one case, Hays defended author Max Bodenheim and his publishers, charged with distributing an obscene book, *Replenishing Jessica*. Hays insisted that the district attorney read the entire book aloud to the jury. The jury, thoroughly bored, acquitted Bodenheim, agreeing with Hays's argument that anything that boring couldn't be obscene.

The ACLU's most famous censorship case involved James Joyce's *Ulysses*. Chapters of the novel, which had been published in Paris, had come out in the American journal the *Little Review* between April 1918 and December 1922. The excerpts stopped appearing when the magazine was prosecuted for publishing obscene matter. "The virulence of the attack was scarcely warranted by the nature of the work," wrote Morris Ernst. Molly Bloom's erotic stream-of-consciousness passages were a minuscule part of the seven hundred-page text—one would have to sift through thousands of words to find anything that would conceivably "corrupt" the reader. Nonetheless, the book stirred up the censors. Copies were burned in England, Ireland, Canada, and the United States. The customs court, calling it obscenity "of the rottenest and vilest character," ordered that all copies coming into the States be confiscated. But the book could be found. One observer noted that "copies of *Ulysses*, carried on the hip, gave young collegiates a kind of prestige comparable to that achieved by a pocket flask." The book was not so much a popular success as a critical one, and by 1932 a number of publishers in America began vying for the privilege of breaking the law in order to publish an American edition. Joyce chose Random House in New York City. Morris Ernst was the publisher's counsel.

Random House arranged to import a copy of the book, which was seized by customs officials, who then brought action in federal court. The case, *U.S. v. One book entitled Ulysses*, was heard by Judge John Munro Woolsey in December 1933. The government's case was lackluster—the attorneys, forced to present a rehash of old-time obscenity scare tactics, were less than enthusiastic. Ernst, meanwhile, was in high form. He held forth on Joyce's brave experiment with language and character, on the foundation of language itself, and the foolishness of censorship. Judge Woolsey, who had spent his summer vacation reading the book, ruled that *Ulysses* was not obscene. He wrote: "Art certainly cannot advance under compulsion to traditional forms and nothing in such a field is more stifling to progress than limitation of the right to experiment with a new technique." Responding to the state's contention that sex occupies too large a part of some of the characters' thought processes, Woolsey said, with admirable humor, "It must be remembered that [Joyce's] locale was Celtic and his season spring." Ernst called the decision "a great stride forward, possibly a greater stride than in any previous case" in the battle against censorship. Ten minutes after he called Random House with the good news, typesetters were at work on the American edition. The book sold thirty-three thousand copies in the first month.

Roger Baldwin was known to be a little squeamish about the public discussion of sex. He was not only more comfortable talking labor, he was more passionate. "However important or significant the defense of religious liberties; of academic freedom; of freedom from censorship of the press, radio, or motion pictures, these are on the whole trifling in national effect compared with the fight for the right of labor to organize." Strong words, backed by strong action. In 1932 Baldwin led the successful fight for the Norris-LaGuardia Act, a law that restricted labor injunctions. But three years later Baldwin balked at supporting the pro-labor Wagner Act. Wagner would create the National Labor Relations Board, and Baldwin, suspicious of government power, felt that the NLRB would invariably side with the employers. The act passed without ACLU help and Baldwin was proved wrong. The Wagner Act emerged as the strongest protection labor had ever known; the right to organize in the workplace, even in the face of employer opposition, was guaranteed.

Even so, in feudal enclaves across the country, local governments denied labor this right. One such enclave was in northern New Jersey. It was called Jersey City, and its mayor was named Frank Hague. "Boss Hague," as most called him, was emperor of a powerful political machine, a labor antagonist, and an ardent suppressor of free speech for anyone who even whispered a favorable word for workers. "Frank Hague was an old time Democratic boss," said Anthony Lewis. "He didn't want the CIO organizing in Jersey City, and he simply banned it."

Whenever a union attempted any sort of meeting in his city, the Boss would declare it "a threat to law and order," and of course it was his sworn duty to uphold order, so the meeting was thereby forbidden. When there were protests about this illegal repression, the Boss replied, "I am the law in Jersey City." During labor actions, Hague's police force arrested picketers under the New Jersey Disorderly Persons Act, a draconian measure that allowed the police to arrest any person "on foot or in any automobile, vehicle or public conveyance who cannot give a good account for himself." It was the perfect strikebreaking tool— picketers went to jail for ninety days under the act. "We hear about constitutional rights, free speech, and free press," Hague said. "Every time I hear these words, I say to myself, 'that man is a Red, that man is a Communist.'"

The Jersey City battle came to a head in 1937. With Morris Ernst directing the legal strategy, the CIO attempted to distribute literature outlining labor's rights under the Wagner Act. Police seized and searched people and automobiles, no warrants necessary. All CIO literature was confiscated, and police routinely searched anyone entering or leaving the CIO offices. According to one report, dozens of men were forced into automobiles and transported outside city limits. The ACLU then attempted to get a permit for an open-air meeting to discuss the Constitution. The permit was denied. When the ACLU's Norman Thomas attempted to speak at one meeting, he was pelted with eggs and Hague had him thrown out of the city. "Jersey City police on horseback broke up the meeting," said the ACLU's Alan Reitman. "They physically lifted up Norman Thomas and threw him down a long flight of stairs which led to the train going back to Manhattan."

Hague's antipathy for labor was shared by many of the good citizens of Jersey City. Pitched battles were fought between CIO workers and members of the American Legion. The Catholic War Veterans announced that if the CIO Reds persisted in invading Jersey City, the veterans would "take the law into their own hands" and throw them out.

But the final victory belonged to labor: the ACLU and the CIO jointly filed suit in the federal district court in Newark for an injunction against such police activities. During the trial the Boss testified, displaying what was, even for those time, an astonishing arrogance. "I think the duty of a mayor," he testified, "is to, from his own observation, ascertain for himself just what's beneficial for the people of the community in which he presides over...I decide. I do. Me." The court ruled in favor of the ACLU. On appeal, Ernst argued the case before the Supreme Court, and won there, too. The decision forced Boss Hague to quit evicting union organizers from the city, stop illegal searches, and stop breaking up union meetings. The duty of the police, the Court ruled, was to *protect* the constitutional right of freedom of assembly, not take it away.

Hague v. *The CIO* "was certainly the epoch-making free speech case of the 1930s," said Anthony Lewis. "It's the first case in which the Supreme Court upheld... the right of organizing. Not just speaking, but organizing labor unions in a city that didn't want them, or a against a city boss who didn't want them." The day after the decision, Boss Hague called up Morris Ernst. He wanted Ernst to draw up "the best free-speech ordinance in the country." With the Boss's backing, Ernst's document passed the city council in five minutes, no questions asked.

The Hague case marked the end of an era. It was one of the last times that the ACLU represented organized labor, for labor no longer needed the help. "Our very close connection with the trade union movement diminished," said Baldwin. "As time went on they took care of themselves." The Hague case was also one of the last examples of ACLU "direct action" for decades. The decision had dissipated Baldwin's skepticism about the courts. A non-lawyer himself, he began to run the ACLU as a sort of sprawling law firm. He directed the work of hundreds of volunteer lawyers and "correspondents"—like-minded libertarians who sent him regular reports on civil liberties issues from all over the country. He added to the growing network of affiliate offices, setting up affiliates in Texas, Iowa, and Indiana. But even as it grew, the organization became more and more identified with Baldwin—as Hays said, "Roger Baldwin *is* the ACLU."

And, in fact, he was. "He could have been a corporate executive at fifty thousand dollars a year," wrote Travis Hoke. "He is director of the American Civil Liberties Union at the wage of a male stenographer." No matter. He had a small private income from his investments, and he lived a very frugal life. "He never gave tips," said his stepson, Carl Baldwin. "Heaven help the taxi driver who took Roger somewhere. I mean if he came away with a dime tip he'd be lucky. And heaven help the waiters."

His marriage to Madeline Doty had, for years, been a non-union. The two spent very little time together. Doty's work with the Women's International League for Peace and Freedom kept her out of the country for months on end. They were with each other, Baldwin once said, only long enough to keep up the "franchise." "She never had any motherly qualities," Baldwin explained. He added, tellingly, "I could have stood a little mothering but I didn't get it from her." The Baldwin-Doty franchise ended in divorce in 1936. That same year he married Evelyn Preston, an heiress with a large personal fortune and two young sons from her first marriage. "They lived in Greenwich Village, in a very nice brownstone," said Alan Reitman. "Whenever you came in he would always introduce you to 'his room,' which was a little side room off the entrance, very sparsely furnished, maybe a wooden bed, a chair, a desk, and that's all. And he said, 'This is where I live.' He wanted to make clear that even though he had resources he was not living high on the hog." Not high on the hog, perhaps, but squarely in the spotlight. He was profiled, quoted, and photographed—he was equally in demand at political meetings and social registry soirées. One writer called him "self-disciplined, aristocratic, Galahadian, full of fervor and violent integrity, emotional, ethical, tirelessly seeking the Grail. A genuine article."

Chapter 7

Slouching Toward the Center:
Anti-Communism in the ACLU

The ACLU, while professing a strong support for the right of all Americans to choose their political philosophies, or to choose to have none, fell victim to Red baiting, to the worst kinds of witch hunting. They just behaved in a disgraceful, disgraceful way.

—Julian Bond

In 1938, Congress relapsed into the patriotic fever it had suffered in 1917. One symptom of this illness was the creation of the House Committee on Un-American Activities (HUAC). Chaired by Martin Dies, the Committee looked for communists everywhere: in the cabinet, in the CIO, in the Campfire Girls. Early in the HUAC hearings, several witnesses mentioned "ACLU" and "communism" in the same sentence. Shortly thereafter, Chairman Dies, in a radio address, claimed that the ACLU was controlled by Communists.

With HUAC set up, Congress next considered a whole new list of loyalty bills. One of them, the Smith Act of 1939, was devised to control alien activity in the United States. The Smith Act made it illegal to advocate overthrow of the government, or to be a member of any organization that advocated the over-throw of the government. The Act regulated admission and deportation of aliens, mandated fingerprinting of all resident aliens, and made it illegal to publish or distribute anti-government literature. It was, said constitutional scholar Zechariah Chafee Jr., "the most drastic restrictions on freedom of speech ever enacted in the United States during peace."

The civil liberties gains of the previous years were undercut by HUAC and the Smith Act. Behind the scenes were even more nefarious goings-on. The FBI, which had played the obe-dient puppy since the Coolidge administration, was maintaining and extending an extensive surveillance network. In 1933, President Roosevelt had instructed J. Edgar Hoover to gather in-formation on the Nazi movement in America and on the do-mestic labor crisis. In 1936, the White House gave the FBI an open mandate for security work—Hoover could thumb his nose at the Justice Department and spy on whomever he chose.

Unaware of the FBI's campaign, the ACLU protested the in-herent injustices of HUAC and the Smith Act. But this was not the ACLU of 1920; the ACLU was now an established political organization with a hard-won position to protect. Their princi-pal cause—the right of labor to organize—had been largely won, and the ACLU found itself drifting into America's main-stream. Baldwin, who enjoyed his small but growing influence in Washington, was becoming very much a centrist in his thinking. One of the key legal minds at the ACLU—Morris Ernst—was fiercely loyal to Roosevelt, who had, after all, signed the Smith Act into law. So although the ACLU protested government's incursions on civil liberties, they did so in a quieter fashion. In fact, while the ACLU protested HUAC's way of doing business, they also sought its favor. Arthur Garfield Hays asked for an op-portunity to go before the Committee and clear the ACLU of any charges brought against it, but Dies refused his offer.

Then came what Baldwin called "the bombshell." On August 23, 1939, Hitler and Stalin signed their non-aggression pact. The Soviet Union, once a beacon of hope for American radicals, had aligned itself with the German Nazis. "That shook Roger Baldwin," said William Donohue. "Roger Baldwin had believed from his earliest of years, right up until that point in 1939, that you could in fact trust the Communists, but you couldn't trust the fascists. What he didn't understand until then is that neither could be trusted." Baldwin, who got the news while vacationing in Martha's Vineyard, immediately resigned from every connection with the Communist Party. "I became a consistent opponent of the Soviet dictatorship, of communism, of all cooperation with communism," he said. Baldwin executed a swift about-face, distanced himself from his former pastimes and former friends, and set out to prove that the ACLU was true-blue American. The first step was to get the HUAC seal of approval. Ernst and Hays visited HUAC in October 1939. They claimed the purpose of the visit was merely to convince the Committee to hear the ACLU rebuttals to charges made against them. But some, including some members of the ACLU board, accused Ernst and Hays of offering to purge the ACLU of communists; HUAC, in return, would pronounce the group above suspicion. The affair remains mysterious. Roger Baldwin always denied it, but it seems possible that a secret deal had been struck. HUAC, in late 1939, issued a statement that directly contradicted its earlier pronouncements on the ACLU. The Union, and Baldwin, were cleared of all "communist connection." At almost the same time, an ACLU sub-committee that included Morris Ernst issued a statement saying that HUAC was performing "a useful and important service." Quite a statement coming from a civil liberties organization, given that HUAC operated with a blatant disregard for the Bill of Rights. The Committee accepted at face the value the shrill and far-fetched testimony of witnesses who fingered, among others, the Boy Scouts and Shirley Temple as communist. It was a forum for Red baiters, pure and simple. But Red baiting was in the air, literally. In an address broadcast over NBC radio, Congressman John J. O'Connor of New York told his listeners: "Always remember the communist tactics are not crude. They are extremely subtle.... The communist action in a democracy is to drive a 'Trojan Horse' in the ranks of unthinking Democrats, and unload its horde of revolutionists at the proper moment."

The next step the ACLU took was more serious. It went on a witch hunt of it own, embarking on what has been called "the one great deviation from principle in its history." Morris Ernst, convinced that communists had infiltrated the liberal movement in America, began a personal campaign to expose communists in two organizations: the ACLU and the National Lawyers Guild. He failed with the Lawyers Guild, and at the ACLU he met with considerable opposition. Board member Corliss Lamont complained that Ernst and other anti-communists on the board made meetings miserable with their constant hammering at the communist issue. Osmond Fraenkel accused Ernst of making "an unworthy attempt to curry favor with Mr. Dies." "The communist virus bit us," recalled Arthur Hays. "The board found difficulty in functioning. Almost every question involving civil liberties would lead to endless discussion."

But Ernst had some strong allies at the ACLU, not the least being Roger Baldwin, who set before the board a number of propositions to deal with the communist "problem." In December 1939 and January 1940, the board narrowly defeated "setting up standards of qualification for membership on the national committee and the board of directors." But on February 5, 1940, the board passed just such a resolution. "It is inappropriate for a member of any organization which supports totalitarian dictatorship" to hold high position in the Union. Read that: "No Communists Allowed." "The resolution merely states what has been always the unwritten policy of the Union," Baldwin claimed, but this was plainly untrue. Several affiliate offices protested, and a few even demanded that the board reverse itself. But Baldwin held firm. "We decided that we couldn't have communists and civil libertarians together. Obviously the loyalty of the communists was to the Soviet Politburo, to the dictatorship. This disqualified them for civil liberties."

But the need for the 1940 Resolution was not obvious to everyone. To this day, the Resolution sparks a heated debate. Ramona Ripston of the ACLU of Southern California said that the resolution was "contrary to what the ACLU stood for." Writer Stanley Fish counters that "what the ACLU was realizing at that moment was that some of the ideas in the marketplace were insidious, being potentially destructive of the marketplace itself. So while purists would condemn the ACLU in retrospect, I would say that is the moment in which the ACLU had its eye on the right question. What are going to be the outcomes?" In fact, some believe that one of the outcomes of the 1940 Resolution was an escalation of repressiveness in the United States. "The so-called 1940 Resolution," said Norman Dorsen, a former president of the ACLU, "really helped pave the way for the excesses of the McCarthy period."

A more immediate outcome, however, was the protest resignation of Harry F. Ward, a founding member of the ACLU and its chairman for years. Ward's leaving shook the other old-timers. Lucille Milner wrote that she felt "shock and sadness at the whole thing." Ward's place was taken by John Haynes Holmes, an avowed enemy of all things communist. Under the terms of the resolution, the members of the staff and governing boards at the ACLU would be "subject to the test of consistency of civil liberties in all aspects and all places." Those who

failed this "test" included anyone who "is a member of any organization which supports totalitarian dictatorship in any
country." To be specific, communists, and more specifically
Elizabeth Gurley Flynn.

Elizabeth Gurley Flynn, at fifty, was a lifelong labor activist
with a history of radical affiliations and a police record to prove
it. She had spent her first night in jail at age sixteen, arrested for
speaking at a Socialist Unity rally in New York's theater district.
She went way back with the ACLU and with Baldwin. She was
a founding member of the Union, and Baldwin's close friend. He
called her "a great girl . . . with a wonderful sense of humor."
They had been true colleagues—when Baldwin took over the
management of the liberal Garland Fund in 1919, he asked
Flynn to serve as one of his trustees. Illness kept Flynn out of political work in the late twenties, but in the thirties she was back
in full force. Always a radical, she joined the Communist Party
in 1936; a year later she sat on its governing board. The Party
was enjoying a growth spurt at the time that Flynn joined. Membership had doubled to eighty thousand in the U.S., and the
Party's coalitions with the liberal groups in the United Front
made it seem far more powerful than it was.

Even after she joined the Communist Party, Flynn stayed on
with the ACLU, and though her membership in the Communist
Party was common knowledge, she had been re-elected to the
board in 1939—unanimously. She was a true field worker, however, often absent from the frequent board and committee meetings held in New York City. At one time she told Lucille Milner
she was afraid of being "squeezed out" of the ACLU because her
work caused her to be gone so much of the time. Baldwin
calmed her fears. "The board needs people who get around the
country in the struggle of the workers."

But after the 1940 Resolution passed, the board requested
Flynn's resignation. Flynn flatly refused to leave, saying that the

board had no right to exclude her solely because of her beliefs. In March, Flynn wrote articles in the *Worker* and *New Masses*, lambasting the ACLU for its position. "I feel like an unwanted wife sent to Reno...except that I don't expect any alimony will be forthcoming....Mr. Roger N. Baldwin used to boast of their broadness, 'Why, we even have a communist on our board,' and the timid old ladies thrilled at his boldness.... Today, they are no longer heretics, non-conformists, radicals— they are respectable....I have seen shadows in the eyes of these nice people, so urbane, so courteous, so 'tolerant,' FEAR OF THE RISING TIDE OF WORKING CLASS POWER. They chop off my head now in the ACLU as a gesture of this fear."

The ACLU retaliated by scheduling a board hearing to address the matter. Three charges were formally filed against her by board member Dorothy Bromley: the first that Flynn, as a communist, was disqualified for a board position at the ACLU; the second and third that the insulting tone of her articles made it impossible for her to continue board membership.

The ACLU bylaws stated that only the board could expel one of its own members, subject to approval of the national committee. Baldwin was director of the ACLU and at board meetings he had a voice, but no vote. Still, there was no question as to the identity of the driving force behind the purge. "Roger Baldwin clearly orchestrated the ouster of Elizabeth Gurley Flynn," said Norman Dorsen. It was, from the start, a sad piece of work on Baldwin's part. He put Bromley up to making the charges for appearances sake. It would look better if a woman pointed the finger at another woman. He denied that this "trial" signaled any change in ACLU policy; his formal line was "no principle was changed." He ignored the fact that Norman Thomas had recently published equally unflattering articles on the ACLU.

The anti-Flynn faction at the ACLU tried to downplay the

whole affair. John Haynes Holmes said that anti-communist sentiment on the board was not new. "There was latent disquiet and a certain uneasiness over a long period of time. Then, last August, on the occasion of Russia's non-aggression pact with Germany, the smouldering beneath the ground suddenly broke the surface and leaped into conflagration."

Flynn had her supporters, both in the Union and outside it. Forty ACLU members resigned in protest of the 1940 Resolution and letters about the Flynn affair from members around the country ran two-to-one in her favor. The Harvard Student Union and the Cambridge Union of University Teachers were opposed to her ouster. But Baldwin had his supporters as well. John Dos Passos, infuriated at the Soviet Union's invasion of Finland, had resigned from the board saying that "as soon as I'm sure the Civil Liberties Union is going to continue the fight for civil liberties which it so magnificently inaugurated during the last war, without the influence of Marxist prejudices, I'll be with you again."

On the night of May 7, 1940, in the City Club of New York, the ACLU Board of Directors held what amounted to a trial. Flynn was present. Baldwin had escorted her there himself, by taxi. Twenty-two of the thirty board members were there; Flynn suspected that at least one member had avoided the trial so as not to go on record voting against her. "This charge," she said, "violates every principle we fought for in the past."

Flynn's position had not changed: the board had no right to expel her because of her beliefs. Furthermore, she did not accept the board's judgment that the Soviet Union was a totalitarian state. Questions were put to her in cross-examination style. Hays asked if her Communist superiors had ever told her how to vote on ACLU matters. Flynn said no. Raymond Wise, to illustrate totalitarian aspects of communism, asked if Party members could openly criticize the party and remain in good standing. It was an ironic question given that, in the case at hand, Flynn was charged with open criticism of the ACLU. Flynn pointed out that the board was, in essence, censoring her speech. "If this trial occurred elsewhere," she said, "it would be a case for the ACLU to defend."

It was an interminable hearing, with lengthy hypothetical discussions about the Communist Party's beliefs regarding liberty. But this was not a theoretical exercise; there was a vote to be taken, and finally, it was. At 2:40 AM, with Flynn out of the room, the board tied—nine for expulsion, nine against. John Haynes Holmes, as chair, broke the tie, and Elizabeth Gurley Flynn was expelled from the ACLU. She was told of the vote informally, by a few board members who joined her after the hearing at the bar of the nearby Algonquin Hotel. When the meeting was over, Baldwin kissed Flynn goodbye. They had been friends for twenty years, and after that night, they never saw each other again. Baldwin had held fast in his determination to expel her. "After the Nazi-Soviet pact," he said, "we would have kicked God himself out."

"A tremendous irony is involved here," said Mary McAuliffe. "Absolutely tremendous. Here's the very organization that should be defending the rights of communists." After the hearing, Baldwin made it clear that the ACLU did not think communists should lose civil liberties—they were simply barred from the leadership of the ACLU. He clung to his "no principle has changed" line. When the national board was polled, twenty-seven voted for expulsion, thirteen against, eleven abstained, and one member wrote to complain of the Star Chamber proceedings that expelled Flynn. The ACLU had conducted a successful witch hunt; it would be followed by a long and bitter season of Red baiting in America.

Only months after the Flynn hearing, Congress passed a law barring communists from employment in certain public agencies, including the WPA. "If the ACLU could do this then there's a precedent certainly for others to do this as well," said Mary McAuliffe. "Not just on the right, but on the left of center. And it became a precedent."

In 1951, the ACLU board institutionalized the 1940 Resolution by making it a permanent part of the ACLU constitution. It was not until 1966 that a movement to repeal the Resolution, initiated by some affiliate offices, finally brought about results— the board established a committee to study the question. In March 1967 the union dropped the statement "the ACLU needs and welcomes the support of all those—and only those—whose devotion to civil liberties is not qualified by adherence to Communist, Fascist, KKK, or other totalitarian doctrine." In April 1968, they rescinded the 1940 Resolution in its entirety. And in April 1976, Elizabeth Gurley Flynn was reinstated on the ACLU board. Oddly, Osmond Fraenkel, the one member board still on the board from 1940, voted against reinstatement. At the 1940 meeting he had voted in Flynn's favor. "The 1940 board was wrong in expelling her, but it's too late to try to right this wrong," he said. "I felt that it was not appropriate for this board to criticize what another board, in another time, did. You can't change history." True. At the time of her reinstatement, Flynn had been dead for twelve years.

"The ACLU is like other organizations in that it's made up of people," said Julian Bond. "And they bring to it their personal and political baggage. The ACLU for years and years carried this rigid anti-communism, expelling Elizabeth Gurley Flynn, just a series of bad behaviors toward people who were Marxist or suspected of being Marxist.... Over years, over time they've done fabulous work. We'd be a poorer country without them and our civil rights and civil liberties would be much less well protected. But they come into this struggle with some awful, awful history, and only recently have begun to dig themselves out."

Chapter 8

The Surrender of Liberty:
The Japanese-American Internment Program in World War II

When we opposed the incarceration of Japanese-American citizens in the early 1940s, we were only one of two national organizations to do so. We were against everybody.
—Ira Glasser

The ACLU of 1941 had at its core a group that was nothing if not tenacious. Twenty-three years after they first came together, Roger Baldwin, Lucille Milner, Arthur Garfield Hays, Morris Ernst, Norman Thomas, and John Haynes Holmes were discussing yet again the troublesome affair that had brought them together in the first place: a world war. If war in 1917 gave the ACLU its start, war in 1941 gave the old-timers a chance to take stock, to measure the progress—or lack thereof—that the country had made in civil liberties. These were people who clearly remembered the cruel treatment of the conscientious objector, the severe limits placed on personal freedom, the fear of all things foreign. "Personally," said Arthur Garfield Hays, "I am not so fearful of what Hitler may do to us as of what he may persuade us to do to ourselves."

There would be no repeat of the disastrous conscientious objector treatment of World War I. Although the Selective Service Act of 1940 did not accommodate the absolutist who refused to perform any type of military service, it did broaden the definition of a CO, and put in place a far more reasonable plan for alternative service. Baldwin set up the National Committee for Conscientious Objectors and the ACLU worked with the group in much the same way that the AUAM had cooperated with the Civil Liberties Bureau in 1918. But in a reversal of his earlier position, Baldwin did not disapprove of the draft itself. "My pacifism," he said, "goes completely under when it comes to defense of democracy against fascism."

In the months leading up to the war, the ACLU had stuck with its policy of defending free speech for German-American Nazis. "Persecute the Nazis," warned one ACLU publication, "and attract to them hundreds of sympathizers with the persecuted who would have otherwise been indifferent." Once war was declared, ACLU board disagreed on the protection this speech deserved, and finally issued a statement saying that not all speech deserved defense in wartime. It was a confused stand for a free speech organization to take, but it was one that was shared by many in the liberal community. Writing in the *Nation*, Freda Kirchwey argued that "tolerance, democratic safeguards, trust in public enlightenment—these happy peace-time techniques have demonstrated their inadequacy.... The Fascist Press in the United States should be suppressed. It is a menace to freedom and an obstacle to winning the war."

The mania for loyalty was quieter this time around, but it was still evident. The government kept up its ongoing loyalty crusade: trials were held under the Smith Act, pro-fascist speech was suppressed, and HUAC assembled an index of "subversives" that numbered more than one million names. However, the government promised to uphold civil liberties even in wartime. Before America entered the war, the Attorney General stated that "an emergency does not abrogate the Constitution or dissolve the Bill of Rights." After Pearl Harbor, President Roosevelt went even further: "We will not, under any threat, or in the face of danger, surrender the guarantee of our liberty our forefathers framed for us in our Bill of Rights." But the government, acting on a direct order from the president, did force the surrender of liberty in a repression campaign unequaled in twentieth-century America. Virtually every organization in America sat and idly watched while the government incarcerated 120,000 Japanese-Americans in concentration camps.

It was a campaign that began quietly. In the days after the Pearl Harbor attack, approximately sixteen thousand foreign nationals, including fourteen hundred Japanese, were detained across the country. More than ten thousand, found to pose no threat to security, were quickly released. The rest, mostly Germans, were detained in camps or, in a few cases, repatriated. A curfew and some travel restrictions were imposed on certain aliens, but in the first weeks no draconian security measures were taken, even in the large Japanese-American communities on the West Coast. Senator Sheridan Downey of California went on the radio to urge his constituents to resist hysteria, reminding them that most people of Japanese ancestry were citizens or longtime residents. Most Nisei—American citizens of Japanese ancestry—in the army were posted to army camps away from the West Coast, and some Nisei lost their government jobs. The mayor of Los Angeles fired thirty-nine Japanese-Americans working for the city, saying that it was impossible for them to prove their loyalty. There were a number of incidents, but no vigilante violence, and no immediate outcry for military action against Japanese-Americans.

At the same time, however, there was a quiet and official movement afoot to isolate all Japanese-Americans or even remove them from the West Coast. The California attorney general and the state's congressional delegation met to discuss the "problem," and called for a strict evacuation policy on the West Coast. Soon others joined in: the Native Sons and Daughters of the Golden West, the Western Growers Protective Association, the American Legion, and the L.A. Chamber of Commerce. With the Japanese navy controlling the Pacific, it was easy to conjure up images of an all-out invasion, or even more frightening, a sabotage campaign in which Japanese saboteurs sneaked into the country and hid themselves amongst the Japanese-Americans living in communities around the West Coast harbor cities. The press chimed in, too. First the Hearst media, then the more liberal dailies, called for some sort of policing of the Japanese-Americans. Conservative columnist Westbrook Pegler trumpeted the most extreme position: "The Japanese should be under guard to the last man and woman," he wrote, "and to hell with habeas corpus."

Astonishingly, he had a disciple in Lt. General John DeWitt, the army's secretary of the Western Defense Command. By late January it was clear in Washington that a sweeping evacuation plan was going to be implemented in the West.

Baldwin learned about the likelihood of a such a plan from his Washington contacts and immediately wrote Ernest Besig in the ACLU's San Francisco affiliate office. The government, Baldwin said, might make "some move" that "would virtually suspend civil liberties." He feared the worst, and rightly so. DeWitt had recommended internment of all people of Japanese ancestry. On February 19, 1942, President Roosevelt signed Executive Order 9066, conferring on the secretary of war the power to designate "military zones" and to exclude "any or all persons" from these areas. DeWitt took charge of the program. The Western portions of Washington, Oregon, and California became Military Zone One; the "any and all persons" excluded from the zone were the Japanese-Americans living there. "Along the vital

Pacific Coast," said DeWitt, "over 112,000 potential enemies, of Japanese extraction, are at large today. There are indications that these are organized and ready for concerted action at a favorable opportunity." In fact, those potential enemies were organized and ready to cooperate to the fullest with any plan that the American government put forth. In San Francisco, according to Besig, the Japanese American Citizen's League "had definitely instructed its people not to contest any action by the local, state, or federal authorities." Nor did they, even when the army ordered that all Japanese-Americans, citizen and alien alike, report to assembly centers for evacuation to areas outside the military zone. There were no individual hearings to find cause for evacuation. The War Relocation Authority (WRA), created to handle the evacuation program, had decided that the presidential war power was broad enough to allow for such a mass evacuation. When it became clear that this large number of evacuees were not going to be welcome anyplace else in the country, the WRA decided that they would be detained, holding that this detention was equally constitutional.

Baldwin felt differently. At the very least, the Fifth Amendment, which prohibits the government from depriving a person of life, liberty, or property without due process, should protect the Japanese-Americans. "We condemned the evacuation the very day we heard about it," said Baldwin, speaking of the ACLU's national office. The ACLU called it "the worst single wholesale violation of civil rights of American citizens in our history." In March, and again in April, Baldwin sent strongly-worded letters to President Roosevelt, arguing that the order deprived citizens of their liberty and use of their property; he likened the assembly and evacuation program to the treatment of the Jews in Europe.

Baldwin laid out a double strategy: first, as with the COs in World War I, the ACLU should try to sway those in power to respect the rights of the evacuees. Baldwin asked for a meeting with DeWitt, but the general ignored the request. He went to Washington to meet with Justice Department officials, and here found Edward Ennis, the head of the Alien Enemy Control Unit, to be sympathetic to the notion that the Japanese-Americans were being deprived of their civil liberties. As Baldwin later explained, the ACLU board in New York "waited for some time to determine what the legal and constitutional issues were to challenge the military authority."

The second step in Baldwin's strategy was to test the legality of Executive Order 9066 in the courts. Baldwin told the California affiliates to find test cases, but none were forthcoming. Even though both affiliates had opposed the order from the beginning, neither had found any evacuee willing to defy the order and go to court. The Japanese-Americans, in their desire to be patriotic, peacefully went along with the government. Eventually, about a dozen people contested the order, but in April 1942 the ACLU had to stand by as the U.S. government removed 112,000 from their homes.

Twenty years earlier, during the Palmer raids, the government had taken motion picture films of the police operation. The footage is nothing less that a sinister version of the Keystone Kops. Mayhem prevails. Men and women are dragged down tenement steps, pinned to the sidewalk, handcuffed, beaten with clubs, and thrown into waiting vans to be taken away. Deportees are loaded onto boats by police escorts and as the deportation ships leave the harbor, the police gaily wave goodbye and good riddance from the docks.

By contrast, the government's filming of the Japanese-American internment yielded footage that is chilling in its order and efficiency. Japanese-Americans report to assembly centers and wait in line to register with the soldiers. Voice-over narration explains that "we are setting a standard for the rest of the world in the treatment of people who may have loyalties to an enemy nation. We are protecting ourselves without violating the principles of Christian charity." The "relocation centers," which were in fact internment camps surrounded by barbed wire and patrolled by armed guards, are presented as "clean, safe, and modern places to live. Many of the new residents will find conveniences at the center that they did not have at home."

The government claimed that detention was a military, rather than a punitive action, but the detention centers were very much like prisons to those who lived there. The centers were hastily-built encampments, thrown together by army engineers in eastern California, Arizona, Colorado, Utah, Idaho, and Arkansas. The lodgings were bleak: wood and tar paper barrack buildings set in barren compounds. The family quarters were furnished solely with bunks and cots. People ate and bathed communally. Although Japanese-Americans cooperated with the program, they did not tolerate such conditions docilely. There was much contention and protest over conditions, and even more protesting about the fact that a Japanese-American man could be drafted from the camp into the army. Bern Friedelson of the New York ACLU was an officer in Military Intelligence during the war, assigned to translate Japanese documents and interrogate Japanese prisoners. "We weren't good enough at Japanese to do the work alone, so Military Intelligence went to the concentration camps . . . and recruited these potential traitors to provide the help we needed."

One center, Tule Lake in northern California, became the segregation center where "disloyal" evacuees were eventually placed. A battalion of armed guards equipped with armored vehicles surrounded the camp. Little wonder that beginning in late 1944 more than six thousand evacuees renounced their American citizenship. "For almost four years," wrote a University of California student hired to observe the effects of evacuation, "the evacuees' experience had been of a nature calculated to make them lose faith in America." Citizenship had become meaningless.

In 1942, Gordon Hirabayashi was a senior at the University of Washington, a Quaker, and a registered conscientious objector; under the terms of Executive Order 9066, he was also a criminal. Beginning in May, Hirabayashi violated the curfew and evacuation orders. When the deadline for assembly had passed, he turned himself in to the FBI office in Seattle. Mary Farquharson, an attorney who had done legal work with Quakers and with the small ACLU organization in Washington state, got wind of Hirabayashi's intention to defy the order. She offered to help him and wrote to Baldwin, asking for support. At last, a test case, and an ideal one. Gordon Hirabayashi was a perfect defendant, a young man of conscience and respectability. His actions in defying the order and then turning himself in mirrored Baldwin's defiance at the draft board some two decades earlier, a fact that further recommended the young man. Baldwin wrote back at once with suggestions for defense attorneys and with an offer of funds: the ACLU would cover the costs of the case. "I hope," he wrote to Farquharson, "your Japanese boy will stick."

Hirabayashi was under some pressure to obey the evacuation order. "My mother wanted me to come with the family to the camp. She said, 'It's a matter of life and death. Why stick to a principle? Stick with us.' She used everything—tears and everything. But I couldn't do it." Despite the pressure, Hirabayashi did "stick"—it was Baldwin, or rather the ACLU, who did not. For although the board had signed Baldwin's early letters to the president, they were very much divided over the executive order. Baldwin, always the diplomat, described the division as "a little debate," but it was in fact a rift of consequence. There were essentially two factions. The first, which included Baldwin,

Norman Thomas, John Haynes Holmes, and Arthur Garfield Hays, questioned the constitutionality of the executive order. The second faction, which included Morris Ernst, did not want the ACLU to come out against the executive order. In this camp there were board members who were blindly loyal to Roosevelt. There were also a few board members who favored the internment program. One board member compared the Japanese-American detention to a public health quarantine for measles.

A referendum was called. On June 16, when all votes were counted, it was clear that Baldwin had lost. The ACLU board overwhelmingly supported the position that the executive order was constitutional; the government, they said, had the right to subordinate civil liberties to military needs. This was by no means a position that excluded all legal questions regarding the internment program. The government could be challenged to show the necessity of the wholesale removal of Japanese-Americans from their homes, and could argue that DeWitt's order unlawfully singled out Japanese-Americans based solely on race. But this was a change from the position outlined in Baldwin's letters to Roosevelt, a change that undercut the Hirabayashi defense. His lawyers laid out a defense based on the unconstitutional nature of Executive Order 9066; it was a defense that ran counter to the ACLU's official position.

On June 22 the board ordered Baldwin to inform the West Coast affiliates that "local committees are not free to sponsor cases in which the position is taken that the government has no constitutional right to remove citizens from military areas." The board also instructed Baldwin to "advise the defendants in the test cases already brought to arrange, if they desire, for counsel who will be free to raise other constitutional issues." Baldwin duly informed Mary Farquharson that the ACLU would not be able to work on the Hirabayashi case. He tried to smooth things over by offering help in raising money for an independent defense committee. Farquharson, deeply disappointed, set about finding other support. Baldwin also alerted Ernest Besig of the San Francisco affiliate, who was now working on a test case for Fred Korematsu, another Japanese-American who had defied the evacuation order. Besig flatly refused to drop the case, and further refused to have it handled by an outside committee. The San Francisco chapter would not withdraw from the Korematsu case, he said. The brief, which directly challenged the executive order, was too far along. When the national board demanded that Besig pursue the case through an independent committee, Besig simply stopped answering their letters.

With the national board divided, Baldwin kept the ACLU closely focused on the aspects of the Japanese-American internment that the ACLU could address. The ACLU was one of the few organization speaking out for the civil liberties of the 112,000 people held in the camps. For the better part of a year, Baldwin kept up pressure at the Justice Department to improve the conditions for the Japanese-Americans, and to develop a release and furlough policy that would ease the economic hardship brought about by detention. He kept channels open with the board at the San Francisco affiliate, and attempted to influence the army's administration of the program. It seems in this last he went too far. When he sent congratulatory letters to General DeWitt, praising the program for its "efficiency," Norman Thomas attacked him as being more agent than gadfly to the army.

Meanwhile, Gordon Hirabayashi sat in a Seattle jail awaiting trial. Frank Walters, the defense attorney that Farquharson had secured for Hirabayashi, was struggling to produce a strong defense, but it was an uphill battle. The judge assigned to the case was Lloyd D. Black, a jurist who made no bones about his support for the internments. The West Coast, he believed, was wide open to attack by Japan. He warned of an "air armada that would rain destroying parachutists from the sky"; presumably these invaders would be aided by Japanese-Americans like Hirabayashi himself.

The trial was held in October. Frank Walters argued that the curfew and evacuation orders violated Hirabayashi's Fifth Amendment rights. The state countered simply by demonstrating that the defendant had violated curfew and evacuation laws. Judge Black instructed the jury "to accept the laws as stated by the court, despite any opinion of your own that the law should be different," in effect telling the jury to return a guilty finding, which they did in ten minutes. The judge sentenced Hirabayashi to thirty days imprisonment for each charge, but at the defendant's request actually lengthened the sentence by changing it to two ninety day sentences to be served concurrently. An odd request, but Hirabayashi wished to serve his time at an outdoor work camp rather than in a jail cell, and had been told that he was unlikely to be assigned to a camp for a sentence shorter than ninety days.

Hirabayashi was not the only Japanese-American to challenge the order, nor was he the only one to be convicted. In San Francisco, Fred Korematsu, represented by the ACLU, was also found guilty, as was Minouro Yasui of Oregon. All three convictions were appealed, but even during the appeal phase the national ACLU stayed aloof, choosing not to file an *amicus* brief during the initial appeal. When the Appeals Court sent the cases directly to the Supreme Court for action, however, the national office was drawn into the legal battle at last. The individual lawyers and defense committees had neither the funds nor the experience needed to argue a case before the high court. The ACLU's Osmond Fraenkel rewrote the brief in two weeks, careful to adhere to the ACLU's stated position on Executive Order 9066. Fraenkel focused on the unlawful racial discrimination of the case. Two *amicus* briefs were submitted. One was by the Japanese

American Citizen League, which argued that the implementation of the executive order was unlawful because of the racism involved in singling out Japanese-Americans. The brief had particularly strong words about General DeWitt's vicious racism. This was a particularly apt argument. DeWitt had recently told a congressional panel that individual hearings were not necessary in the internment order because "a Jap's a Jap." Baldwin welcomed the JACL's brief, but exploded at the second brief, submitted by the San Francisco affiliate. The San Francisco brief attempted to browbeat a reversal out of the Supreme Court—it compared DeWitt to Attila the Hun, and demanded that the Hirabayashi conviction be overturned. It also contested the constitutional authority of the executive order, running counter to the ACLU's directive. Baldwin, thoroughly disgusted, threatened the affiliate with disaffiliation. An apology from the director of the San Francisco board eventually calmed things down, but the brief underscored a problem that the ACLU would face again: how to manage an unruly affiliate chapter.

The Supreme Court heard arguments on all three cases on May 10, 1943. The defense lawyers, citing equal protection and unlawful delegation of power to the military, asked that the Court reverse the convictions. Al Wirin of the Southern California ACLU told the Justices that "neither race nor color has any military significance." After the arguments, some of the attorneys felt optimistic, but in the Court's deliberation, Chief Justice Harlan Stone firmly guided the Court to a unanimous decision that upheld Hirabayashi's original conviction for curfew violation. Stone had the Court sidestep the whole issue of unlawful detention. Hirabayashi had received two concurrent sentences, the first for curfew, the second for violation of the evacuation order. Stone claimed that the Court need not deal with the second issue; the concurrent nature of the sentence rendered it moot. The record shows that several of the Justices questioned aspects of the order as it was carried out against the Japanese-Americans, but there was no formal dissent to the decision. It was, said the ACLU's Burt Neuborne, "the lowest the Court has sunk in the twentieth century."

Gordon Hirabayashi had been out on bail; the Supreme Court decision sent him back to prison. Picked up by FBI agents while mowing the lawn, Hirabayashi was ordered to report to the Spokane County jail. When he asked to be sent to an outdoor prison camp, the agents refused. The only nearby camp was in a restricted area; the other was in Tucson, and there was no money to send him there. When Hirabayashi offered to get there on his own, the agents agreed. He spent several days hitchhiking to Arizona, only to be told that the camp had no papers on him. Hirabayashi told the federal marshal that someday the papers would be found, and that he would have to serve the time eventually, "so you might as well find them and get this over with." The papers were found, and Gordon Hirabayashi served out the balance of his sentence. "The funny thing," he recalled later, "is that the camp was in a restricted area, but they let me stay there anyway."

"We believe," wrote Yale law professor Eugene Rostow in 1945, "that the German people bear a common responsibility for outrages secretly committed by the Gestapo and the SS. What are we to think of our own part in a program which violates every principle of our common life, yet has been approved by the President, Congress, and the Supreme Court?" It took thirty-five years to answer that question. In 1980, Congress established a blue-ribbon Commission on Wartime Internment and Relocation of Civilians, and took the testimony of more than seven hundred witnesses. The commission concluded the program had been wrong from the start: racially biased, punitive, and built on trumped-up threats to national security. The commission placed responsibility at the highest level: President Roosevelt, Secretary of War Stimson, and General DeWitt. In 1988, Congress passed a restitution bill. By way of compensation, each survivor of the internment camps was given twenty thousand dollars. "President Reagan, surely no friend of the ACLU, signed that bill," said Ira Glasser. "The bill said the internment of the Japanese-Americans in the early 1940s was an act of racism and war hysteria—almost exactly the words that the ACLU had used forty years before."

"I never look at my case as just my own, or just as a Japanese-American case," said Gordon Hirabayashi. "It is an American case, with principles that affect the fundamental human rights of all Americans."

Chapter 9

Making the Right Noises:
The ACLU Response to McCarthyism

Opposition to communism becomes a kind of secular American religion. And every initiative, foreign and domestic, is weighed against whether or not it furthers or hinders the communist menace. And the ACLU fell victim to this.

— *Julian Bond*

"Regretfully we are obliged to share with you our financial problems. Here they are..." The fundraising letter of January 1948 laid out the ACLU's money troubles. Their many cases—defending labor's rights under the Taft-Hartley Act, defending the rights of racial minorities, protecting federal employees from unfair dismissal—were proving costly. At the same time, some of their eight thousand members had failed to send in their renewal checks. To impress these errant donors and to lure a few new ones into the fold, the ACLU enclosed a number of press clippings from some of their more successful and popular cases. The most telling is dated June 23, 1947: "The Civil Liberties Union is today standing guard over the rights of a free people in the face of a developing hysteria for an all-out witch-hunt." A strong and reassuring statement that is contradicted two sentences later. The ACLU "insists that the legitimate job of exposing communists and weeding them out of federal service be conducted with full safeguards for those accused."

That the American Civil Liberties Union considered "exposing communists" a "legitimate job" is, in hindsight, startling, but at that time not surprising at all. The Truman administration's Federal Loyalty Program, set up in 1947 to keep communists out of the federal workplace, was a popular program, well-received by political organizations and the public. Even the ACLU approved of the loyalty oath required of federal employees under the program, raising only faint protests about blacklisting and fairness. In fact, loyalty programs proliferated, to the general approval of Americans. A 1948 Gallup Poll showed that 63 percent of those polled favored the Mundt-Nixon Bill, which would require individuals with communist connections to register with the Justice Department. A 1949 poll showed that 80 percent favored the law that required labor leaders to swear they were not communists before they brought a case before the National Labor Relations Board. Eventually, thirty-two states would require loyalty oaths of teachers, and twenty-seven states would adopt laws keeping "subversives" off the ballot. In 1953, Utah was the only state in the Union without some sort of loyalty or communist registration law on its books.

"Many Americans," said Anthony Lewis, "were afraid of the Soviet Union. It wasn't a totally irrational fear. Soviet-armed guerrillas had threatened Greece, and eventually Soviet-sponsored politicians took over in Czechoslovakia and then in Hungary. These were realities. But Americans frightened of communism abroad directed their fear to communism at home, which was completely unfrightening. The Communist Party probably consisted of 702 people, 680 of whom were actually FBI agents. I mean that as a joke, but there was lot to it."

Fear of communism cropped up in the courts as well as in public opinion polls. In 1948, after a year-long secret session, a federal grand jury handed down Smith Act indictments against a dozen Communist Party leaders. The charge: "Conspiring to advocate the overthrow of the government," which, in essence, meant that the Party members were indicted for planning to talk about bringing down the government. The charge was peculiar to say the least, but with no real evidence of treason, the prosecution had to find a creative way of bringing the Communists to trial. The ACLU, "motivated only by our concern for civil liberties," announced its intention to enter the case. Baldwin was eager to fight this blatant attack on free speech, but unwilling to take the unpopular path of defending communists directly. Thus he called for "an attack on the constitutionality of the Smith Act and an indictment which, on its face, in our judgment violates every principle of the freedom of speech and press." The Union demanded that the indictments be dropped, and then filed an *amicus* brief on behalf of the defendants, careful all the while to keep their arguments focused on constitutional issues. It was, as historian Mary McAuliffe said, "definitely a more conservative approach, a more cautious approach."

"We made the right noises during that period," said Burt Neuborne, "but we refused to directly represent any of the people who were involved in those cases, in large part because they were communists and because the organization didn't want to be publicly perceived as linking itself with communists. And so we tried to stay at arm's length and to simply file briefs on their behalf but not to really get in the mud and roll around."

After a stormy, nine-month trial in New York City, eleven defendants were found guilty of conspiracy and received jail terms ranging from three to five years. The judge also found the defense attorneys in contempt of court—a measure that made it difficult for communists to find legal representation in other cases. During the appeal, Arthur Garfield Hays and Osmond Fraenkel wrote an ACLU *amicus* brief that argued for a reversal of the conviction. The Smith Act was a violation of the First Amendment, they argued. "Even if constitutional," the brief went on, "the statute applied to the eleven is invalid because it was applied in the absence of a jury finding of a clear and present danger."

"During the anti-communist years," said Chuck Morgan of the ACLU, "the ACLU used to file *amicus curiae* briefs, friend-of-the-court briefs. It was a way to avoid all controversy, to defend a principle, not a human being. It's like writing a letter to the court and saying, 'Hi there, court, let us tell you why you should rule our way on the Constitution.'" Neither the appeals court nor the Supreme Court ruled the ACLU's way in this case. The Supreme Court found that "clear and present danger" did exist, and the convictions were upheld. "Anyone who took the civil liberties protections of the Constitution for granted got quite a rude shock in the cold war," said Anthony Lewis. "The Supreme Court, under the stress of those times, was not prepared to defend what we today would think of as deserving protection."

Corliss Lamont, a longtime member and a big-time funder of the ACLU, grew tired of the Union's timidity in the face of the Smith Act prosecutions. He organized the Emergency Civil Liberties Committee. Its purpose was to "augment the American Civil Liberties Union, but with guts enough to fight the evils of McCarthyism without fear." The ECLC, which, in 1997, merged with the Center for Constitutional Law, was never as large or as well-known as the ACLU. But its chief counsel, Leonard Boudin, did take on direct representation of clients that the ACLU simply would not touch. "There was that feeling," said Norman Dorsen, "that we were not as active as we should have been. But remember, our function as a civil liberties organization was to be interested in more than just one particular issue. We had church-state separation cases, police brutality cases, racial discrimination cases."

The ACLU did, in fact, have a broad agenda. They were involved in labor disputes, fair housing cases, and free speech cases. The 1949 Annual Report voiced hopes for a UN-sponsored International Bill of Rights. This last was a pet cause of Baldwin, who was always interested in getting the Union to extend its reach beyond the U.S. borders. A few years earlier he had gone to Japan and South Korea, at the request of General Douglas MacArthur, to render his opinion on the democratization programs in those countries. It was a role Baldwin relished: an international advisor to the man who had won the war in the Pacific. On his return he held forth on Korea's problems—"The middle-of-the-road is conspicuous by its absence. We were unable to find a democratic center"—and waxed eloquent on Japan's bright prospects. "Democracy in Japan is an uplifting experience," he said. "It is a crusade." Clearly, he loved this kind of extracurricular work. Shortly, he would find himself with plenty of time to do more of it.

At an afternoon board meeting in 1950, Roger Baldwin staged a filibuster at the ACLU. At sixty-six years old, he was trying to stave off the inevitable. Eventually a board member interrupted: "Everyone knows why we're here." Baldwin sat down in a corner, dejected, as the board recommended "that Roger Baldwin be entirely relieved from executive responsibilities." In later versions of the story, Baldwin claimed that he had been looking forward to the change, but the minutes of that meeting make it clear: the ACLU had kicked its founder upstairs.

There were a number of reasons for the board to take such a radical step. Several people were tired of Baldwin's management practices, which included the short leash and tight budget. He could be witty and charming, but he could also work his staff mercilessly, pay them badly, and fire them frequently. "I went to see Roger Baldwin in 1949," said Alan Reitman. "There was a position open at the ACLU for director of public information and public education. I was hired. I was the fifteenth director of public information that Roger had in two years." There were others who realized that Baldwin could no longer control the contentious board, and that the ACLU, mired in conflict about its stance on communism, had to make a change.

Retirement in no way separated Baldwin from the organization he had founded three decades before. He chaired the national committee and was given the official title of "International Advisor" to the ACLU. "We are sure," editorialized one writer in the *Nation*, "that Mr. Baldwin will keep a fatherly eye on the organization so that it may continue to flourish and carry on the fight in a period when human rights in America are more cheaply held than at any time since the dark days following World War I."

"Did he really step down from the ACLU?" said his stepson, Carl Baldwin. "No. He stayed very close. And I think he went to the monthly meetings of the board or whatever. He kept coming and I'm sure he kept expressing his opinion. And I'm sure that for some of these leaders it was very tough to have the great man trooping in every month telling them where to get off." Baldwin kept his own office at the ACLU, from which he dispensed advice to any who asked and to many who didn't. "I was a young lawyer, I had just been hired by the organization," said Burt Neuborne. "I would get into the office in the morning and the telephone would ring. And after a while I began to realize it was Roger by the sort of crackling and breathing on the phone. He hated to speak on the phone, so everything was to be done quickly. He would bark out a series of orders about what needed to be done that day because he would have read the *Times* or read the *Washington Post*, been enraged about some injustice somewhere, and gotten on the phone to get us to fix it. Each morning I would come in and there would this be this voice from the past. It would be Roger Baldwin, the legend, speaking directly to me, saying 'fix it.'"

After Baldwin, said Norman Dorsen, "the organization changed to a very, very different model from the one he had in mind. Baldwin thought of the ACLU as a group of elitists, of highly educated people, a few thousand at most throughout the country, who would be the vanguard of a movement to protect individual rights in this society. But the view of the people who came after him, and the view today, is that the ACLU can and should be a mass movement, that we should not be limited to five, ten, or fifteen thousand people." Baldwin's successor, Patrick Murphy Malin, had been an economics teacher at Swarthmore since 1930, but was also vice-director of the Intergovernmental Committee for Refugees in World War II, vice-chair of the American Friends Service Committee, president of the National Council on Religion in Higher Education, and a consultant to the State Department on foreign affairs. Malin's gift was for administration. He ran a tight, efficient, productive office, and did a brilliant job of increasing membership—the ACLU had about eight thousand members in 1950 and more than thirty thousand in 1955. But Malin was not nearly so comfortable as Baldwin in the shifting, amorphous political world. He lacked Baldwin's dynamism and confidence. He sought the board's approval on every move, an unfortunate way of doing business, since the board he had inherited was fractious and divided. There were old-timers who missed Baldwin and newcomers determined to make their mark; there was also the perpetual pitched battle over communism. "The ACLU," said Mary McAuliffe, "spent so much of its time debating, discussing, fighting over how the organization would establish and maintain its anti-communist credentials that it was being diverted from its main task." During Malin's tenure at the Union, the American Legion constantly attacked the Union, calling it a Communist front. At the same time, the ECLC and several ACLU affiliates demanded Malin take stronger action against the anti-communist crusade that was ripping the country apart.

"The Communist Party in the United States was never strong enough to be a menace at any time," Roger Baldwin later recalled. "Anti-communism was much more of a menace to civil liberties." If the communists were weak, the House Committee on Un-American Activities was more powerful than ever. Congress consistently voted it the funds to continue holding hearings. In fact, between 1950 and 1956, there was not a single instance in which there were more than two votes against HUAC's appropriation. Using this money and its amassed political clout, HUAC launched an assault on the political liberty of Americans—probably the most extreme attack on freedom of speech in our history. "HUAC," said Alan Reitman, "was a major threat not only because of what it did because but also because of what it symbolized. Here was a governmental body, an entity of the United States Congress, whose mandate was to investigate propaganda and subversive activities. Well, propaganda basically means speech, and speech means ideas and opinions. Therefore the United States Congress was telling one of its agencies to look into what people thought, wrote, and said. It was a direct affront to the First Amendment."

In the early 1950s, other investigating committees were born and flourished. Senator Joseph McCarthy of Wisconsin brought his own vicious brand of witch hunting to America. McCarthy, whose initial foray into anti-communism was a re-election campaign strategy rather than a heartfelt commitment to national security, targeted communism in government. His style was reckless and his methods remarkably sloppy. In his opening charges about communists in the State Department, he brandished a list of names of alleged communist sympathizers in the government, sometimes claiming there were 205 names, other times that there were 57 or 81. But McCarthy rode the wave of anti-communism to power. In 1952, he became the chair of the Senate Committee on Government Operations. He called Baldwin a "draft dodger," and read a report aloud in Congress that charged the ACLU's retired leader with communist sympathies. It was a charge that worried some at the ACLU. "The Joe McCarthy period was a bad one," said Baldwin. "It was the worst. McCarthy whipped up anti-communist sentiment all over the country to such a degree that people were suspicious that neighbors down the street were communist. Anybody who had a different view was likely to be communist."

Newsreel footage from 1953 shows McCarthy racing through hearing after hearing, witness after witness. In trademark style, he fired off questions, then banged his gavel whenever a witness tried to give an answer more detailed than "yes" or "no." One such exchange is typical:

> McCarthy: "Do you know the man, or do you not know the man? Just answer the question."
>
> Witness: "You have called me here, I've been here since ten o'clock this morning, now when I try to answer..."
>
> McCarthy: "Will the bailiff remove the witness from the room."

"He was not," said Anthony Lewis, "a sincere anti-communist. He would carry on in this rabid way in front of the television cameras, but when filming would stop, he'd go off and put his arm around some person he'd just been screaming at—or some journalist who he knew disapproved, like me—and say 'let's have a drink.' It was game, a political game that produced some really terrible things."

Actress Betty Garrett attests to this description of McCarthy. After she and her husband had been blacklisted, the only entertainment work they could find was in Las Vegas shows. One night Joe McCarthy, who was in the audience, invited them to his table for a drink. "We were astonished," said Garrett. "We went to his table, because we couldn't believe he would really do this. But there he was, acting as if he was our best friend. We both made a very quick exit."

"One of the by-products of the Red scare," said Anthony Lewis, "was the deep concern of liberal organizations lest they be infiltrated by communists. That was true of labor unions, it was true in the arts, and it was true in the ACLU." In the 1940s, the ACLU's Morris Ernst had been convinced that communists were out to take over America's liberal organizations. He set out to stop them, beginning by lobbying for legislation that would require all organizations seeking postal privileges to disclose the names of all officers and donors, making it impossible for individuals to support a controversial cause anonymously. "There is immediate need for the light of day on all those selling ideas to our public," Ernst wrote. "The Bill of Rights negates the need of anonymity." But his proposed law pleased no one. The Right wanted something much stronger, the Left wanted no part of any law that would increase the government's power. The legislation failed, but Ernst pushed ahead with his anti-communist crusade, maintaining a twenty-six-year correspondence with J. Edgar Hoover. Between 1939 and 1964, Ernst and Hoover exchanged more than three hundred letters, oddly cordial on the part of both men, and oftentimes fawning on Ernst's part. Much of the information Ernst passed on to Hoover was insignificant, some of it little more than gossip. He forwarded ACLU materials and shared information about decisions taken at ACLU board meetings. A 1977 ACLU inquiry into the affair found the arrangement free of "overt improprieties," but the letters shed a very unflattering light on the ACLU's general counsel. He often sent Hoover copies of letters he had received from other people, third-party letters from associates who had no idea that their correspondence would make its way into the FBI files.

Ernst made no secret of his admiration for Hoover, nor did he hide the fact that he stood ready to help the Bureau. Journalist Harrison E. Salisbury wrote that Ernst "took a position that may seem curious today: the FBI was a simple collector of raw data, just like a vacuum cleaner, really." That Ernst truly believed that Hoover and his Bureau were neutral fact-finders demonstrates a naiveté of the first magnitude on the part of a brilliant lawyer, one who can be credited with some of the most important censorship and labor victories of the twentieth century. "The significance," wrote Salisbury, "lies in what it reveals about the state of civil liberties and its flawed defenders at that time."

Baldwin, too, was naive when it came to the FBI. "For quite a number of years," he said later, "we had no difficulty with Mr. Hoover. As a matter of fact, I saw him half a dozen times. And much of the complaints that we had about FBI men he handled rather diplomatically. But it turned out to be false. Mr. Hoover was a real menace, a sort of a political policeman. He established a political secret service, and we didn't know much about it." In fact, the ACLU knew almost nothing about the fact that Hoover, from 1924 on, kept the ACLU under steady surveillance. After 1924, when Harlan F. Stone had supposedly reformed the Bureau, Hoover simply took his spying underground. He instructed his agents to gather information on Baldwin and on the ACLU, and over the years, FBI field agents sent in thousands of pages of information. One FBI agent successfully infiltrated an affiliate executive board in California. Ironically, the national office of the ACLU routinely defended the FBI from its detractors. When the Philadelphia ACLU affiliate office wanted to distribute a pamphlet advising people about their rights during FBI questioning, the national office objected. But Hoover was unimpressed with these shows of loyalty and he kept the Union under close surveillance for years.

In 1954, the communist witch hunt showed the first signs of running out of steam. Joe McCarthy loved the television camera, so it is fitting that it was television that helped undo him, simply by broadcasting his reckless hearings. In March, McCarthy's subcommittee opened hearings to investigate the army. The army retaliated, charging that McCarthy had sought preferential treatment for one of his former aides, recently drafted. In response, McCarthy accused the army of pressuring him to suspend hearings on communist infiltration. The hearing was broadcast in installments, and the American public was treated to a month-long show of McCarthy's crude style and tactics. Presented by Edward R. Murrow, and later distributed as the documentary *Death of a Witch Hunter*, the footage showed McCarthy being caught red-handed falsifying photographic evidence. The senator attempted to regain control of the hearing by attacking a young associate of the army counsel, an insufferable maneuver that prompted the disgusted army counsel to ask, "Have you no sense of decency, sir?" The exchange led to an abrupt adjournment of the hearing, and as the crowd filed out, McCarthy ranted on to an emptying room and to a television audience of twenty million viewers. The end was near for America's preeminent witch hunter. In December 1954, he was officially censured for his activities by the United States Senate. He died three years later.

The motion picture camera contributed to the undoing of HUAC in a similar fashion. In 1960, HUAC, working with a Washington, D.C., film company, released *Operation Abolition*, a forty-five-minute film showing protests of a HUAC hearing in San Francisco. HUAC's chair, Francis E. Walter, introduces the film: "During the next few minutes, you will see revealed the longtime, classic communist tactics in which a relatively few well-trained, hard-core communist agents are able to incite and use non-communist sympathizers to perform the dirty work of the

Communist Party." In this case, the "sympathizers" were Berkeley students, protesting the three days of HUAC hearings being held in San Francisco. On the second day of protests, the San Francisco police turned fire hoses on the students. The resultant mayhem was filmed by local television stations and the same footage was subpoenaed and used to make the film. According to the film, communist agitators were in the Bay Area to carry out "Operation Abolition," a plot to overthrow HUAC and the FBI. The film was heavily edited—events were shown out of the sequence, and subpoenaed witnesses were presented as agitators coming to the hearings solely to incite riot. Two thousand copies of the film were sold, but its wide distribution did not have the desired effect. The *Washington Post* called the movie "a forgery by film." The *Christian Century* called it "a startling piece of propaganda," full of "inaccuracies and distortions."

The Northern California affiliate got hold of *Operation Abolition* and released their own version, *Operation Correction*. Using the same footage, the narrator challenged the HUAC version of events. "We're going to play fair, the American way," said the film's narrator. "We don't think you answer lies and propaganda with more propaganda. We think that if we show you the original film, with the same sequences in it, in the same positions, but tell you in straight simple facts on which date each sequence was made, you'll see what occurred in San Francisco." The film graphically demonstrated that HUAC had manipulated the facts to suit their own story.

The affiliate offices were tiring of the national office's reticence in the face of continued HUAC intimidation. At the 1960 Biennial Conference, the Southern California Civil Liberties Union sponsored a resolution making the abolition of HUAC "a prime order of business." A few years earlier, the national ACLU had said that any campaign to abolish HUAC would be "pointless." Now, with the affiliates demanding action, and the public angered at HUAC's misdeeds, the ACLU finally changed its mind. Working in conjunction with the affiliates, they began a lobbying campaign to convince Congress to vote against funding for the committee. The money stopped and so did the hearings. The final vestiges of HUAC disappeared completely in 1975. HUAC's demise was a clear victory for the California affiliates, and a clear signal to the national office of the ACLU: the defense of civil liberties required a return to the trenches.

Chapter 10

An Explosion of Rights:
The ACLU in the 1960s

The white South owned every judgeship, every prosecutor,
almost every defense attorney, and almost every jury. And the
only place that a black person fit in the court system in the
South was as a janitor or as a defendant.

—Chuck Morgan

In 1966, the ACLU docket was loaded with cases that ten years earlier they simply would not have touched. The once-stodgy Union was representing draft card burners, attacking the mandatory loyalty oath imposed on Medicare recipients, and challenging the death penalty. In Alabama and Mississippi, the ACLU was fighting the age-old practice of jury segregation; in Virginia, they had taken on the case of several students denied entry to a state school because they wore beards. "Grooming," said the ACLU, "is another form of self-expression." Baldwin continued to tinker whenever possible with the day-to-day business of the Union, but he could no longer dictate its every move.

That same year, eighty thousand people paid six dollars apiece for the privilege of calling themselves ACLU members. The staff was still relatively small—fewer than one hundred salaried workers nationwide. But there were many times that number of volunteers, for the most part "cooperating" attorneys, volunteering on cases the ACLU deemed worthy of support. The annual budget was 1.4 million dollars, but the volunteer services were easily worth triple that amount. The organization's third executive director, John Pemberton Jr., took an activist's view of his organization's role. "There's often a wide gap," he said, "between the liberties America proclaims and the things America does. The Union's purpose is to close that gap."

The newly-energized ACLU took much of its inspiration from the civil rights movement, which, according to the ACLU's Jay Miller, "set off the explosion of rights in this whole country. Things opened up not only for African-Americans, but for everybody. Women, other minorities, eventually gays latched onto it." But how the ACLU connected with the civil rights movement in the first place can be summed up in two words: Chuck Morgan.

In September 1963, Chuck Morgan, a successful young lawyer in Birmingham, Alabama, made an impassioned speech at that city's Young Business Club. The day before, four young black girls had been murdered in a bombing at the Sixteenth Street Baptist Church. Morgan laid the blame for their deaths squarely on the shoulders of middle-class white citizens, who had for years tolerated racism in their community. "The theme of the speech," said Morgan, "was 'who threw that bomb?' The answer should have been 'We all did.'" The speech marked the end of Morgan's Birmingham law career. His house was spray-painted with swastikas and KKK symbols and "nigger lover" was scrawled on the siding. Sinister warnings came by mail and by telephone; Morgan's secretary found herself politely handling death threats at the office.

Morgan and his family were forced to leave Birmingham. He set up practice in Virginia and took on cases for the NAACP's Legal Defense Fund. In 1964, Pemberton recruited him to run the ACLU's newly-opened Southern Regional Office in Atlanta, an office Ira Glasser described as "an outpost of civil liberties." ACLU membership topped out at under three thousand in the South. Of the eleven states that make up the region, only two had any ACLU presence at all. "The first time I met Roger Baldwin was at an ACLU board meeting," Morgan later recalled. "I was introduced and he said, 'Oh, yes, you're the young man that we're sending south. We sent a man south many years ago. What was his name? Whatever happened to him?" But the ACLU was not really sending Morgan south. As Jay Miller put it, "Chuck Morgan really brought the South to us."

Morgan also brought the ACLU a unique set of civil rights cases, including a landmark jury segregation case and a legislative apportionment case that resulted in the "one person, one vote" ruling in the South. "In the middle 1960s," said Julian Bond, "any lawyer, white or black, who took these civil rights cases, civil liberties cases, was putting his life and reputation at risk." Morgan took on the risk with relish. He did, according to Bond, travel with a pistol for a time, but he made no effort to keep a low profile. "When Chuck would walk through an airport," said Norman Siegel, "he'd say hi to everyone. It would be 'how you doin', ma'am?' 'How you doin', sir?' A lot of the ACLU people were introverted. Morgan was the opposite. He was outgoing. He would shake anyone's hand." "Chuck Morgan," said Ira Glasser, "is loud and funny and imaginative and audacious, and, you know, he is the best trial lawyer I have ever seen."

In 1965, Morgan filed a stream of lawsuits in the Deep South, demanding an end to the time-honored practice of excluding blacks from southern juries. It was a practice that literally allowed whites to get away with murder. White juries simply did not convict their own when the victims were black. Statistics bore this out: of fifty-eight race murders committed in the South since 1955, only six had ended in conviction. Morgan's crusade was based on his belief that jury reform was as important as the vote to the civil rights movement. "There are only two instrumentalities of power," he told one reporter, "the vote and the jury. How easy is it to cast a ballot when you're afraid that someone, from the sheriff on down, might shoot you and nobody will do anything about it?" One suit—titled *White* v. *Crook* because of Morgan's clever manipulation of the names of the black plaintiffs and white county officials—charged that juries in Hayneville, Alabama, had been systematically segregated by race and by sex. The Justice Department agreed, coming in on Morgan's side in federal court. In February 1966, the court ruled for Morgan's argument—discrimination was unconstitutional. "I don't find fault with the jury system," said Morgan. "I just think we ought to try it sometime."

In Atlanta, on January 6, 1966, John Lewis of the Student Non-Violent Coordinating Committee issued a statement that read in part: "We are in sympathy with, and support, the men in this country who are unwilling to respond to a military draft which would compel them to contribute their lives to United States aggression in Vietnam in the name of the freedom we find so false in this country." Julian Bond, aged twenty-six, a SNCC officer recently elected to the Georgia House of Representatives, endorsed the statement, which was, in the minds of many, an inflammatory piece of work. The *Atlanta Constitution* attacked the SNCC resolution, and by inference Bond, as anarchistic, even treasonous. The statement, said the paper, "went far beyond dissent." The Georgia House of Representatives, led by Representative Jones Lane, immediately decided that the endorsement disqualified Bond for office and took measures to deny Bond the seat he had won with 82 percent of the votes from the 136th district. A SNCC member called Chuck Morgan at the ACLU's office in Atlanta. Morgan took the case at once. It was, he said, "a surefire winner." Bond, who was also represented by his brother-in-law, Howard Moore, called the ACLU intervention in the case "manna from heaven."

"Julian Bond," said Morgan, "was representing a new generation to be seated in the Georgia House of Representatives. The legislature decided that, based on his political views, they had the right to overrule the voters in his district who had elected him in a free, fair, and open election. Now, it struck me that that had something to do with the Constitution of the United States." This was a First Amendment case, similar to that of the five Socialists who had been drummed out of the New York legislature in 1920. But as Bond said later, "I'm sure my race had something to do with it."

In fact, race had everything to do with it. Bond, as a black man, was an absolute affront to the racist sensibilities in the Georgia legislature. Julian Bond was intelligent, educated, unafraid to speak his mind—in short, the type of black man most detested by white racists in the South. The SNCC was equally anathema—an organization that had successfully marched against segregation in the South and in doing so had effectively exposed the brutal ways of segregation to the rest of the nation. Finally, there was Morgan himself, a white southerner in seersucker who should have sided with the legislature, but was instead allied with the ACLU. As Bond later put it, "Morgan took a great risk in associating with this liberal organization, this Yankee organization coming down to upset the southern way of life."

That January, Lester Maddox, who had once pointed a gun at blacks seeking to be served in his restaurant, roamed the halls of the Georgia State House, campaigning for governor in the upcoming election. The Georgia House of Representatives assembled for their swearing-in ceremony, the members wearing little tin American flags on their lapels to mark the occasion. Before the ceremony commenced, Bond was told to sit down. "I will ask Representative Bond to remain seated while I administer the oath of office," said the presiding judge. "Will all members with the exception of Mr. Bond please rise, raise your right hand, and repeat after me..." Bond sat quietly while the others pledged to "support the constitution of this state and the United States." The House clerk then told Bond to step outside. Bond had been asked to leave the Georgia House once before— several years earlier he had been expelled from the visitors' gallery when he refused to sit in the Jim Crow section. This time, as he left, he was swarmed by reporters. In a prepared statement he said: "The fact of my election to public office does not lessen my duty or desire to express my opinions, even when they differ with those held by others."

The Georgia House moved quickly to deal with the matter, setting up a special twenty-eight-man committee to hear the evidence and report to the full House "before nightfall." Denmark Groover, counsel for the challenging legislators, asked Bond if he still endorsed the statement. "I do," replied Bond. A number of character witnesses attested to Bond's loyalty, and Chuck Morgan, with a copy of the state's constitution in his pocket, addressed the assembly. A *New York Times* report said Morgan's voice quavered with emotion and "his great hulk arched over the rostrum." "If Mr. Bond has committed treason, then the proper place for Mr. Bond to be tried is in a court of law. But that is not what this is all about. This issue here is the right of every Georgian to speak."

"To see Morgan in the well of the Georgia House," said Bond, "speaking in a cornpone southern drawl to this audience of cornpone southern legislators just made me know everything was going to be all right." But when the legislators were polled, only twelve voted to give Bond the seat. All were from the Atlanta area and five of them were African-American. Things were not all right. Bond was ousted, and his constituents were left without representation.

The day after the hearing, Governor Sanders congratulated the legislature for acting on the issue "with dignity and a proper sense of responsibility by all concerned....This is as Georgians would have it done." The more conservative black community wanted Bond to somehow smooth over the incident and assume his seat in the house, but Morgan, speaking at the Hungry Club, a Negro luncheon group in Atlanta, claimed that Bond could not get into the legislature unless he crawled in crying, "Massa, Massa, I'se come back."

Julian Bond now took his case to the courts—both federal court and the court of public opinion. The Georgia House had unwittingly ushered Bond onto the national stage: he appeared on television and became a sought-after speaker on the college circuit. The legislature had also given the civil rights movement a rallying cry. The SNCC and the Southern Christian Leadership Conference were unified in their support for Bond. The case, said one writer, "created a new sense of unity in the Negro community...a unity that increasingly sees continuation of the Vietnam war as a threat to American freedom at home." Representatives of fifteen African nations met with Dr. Martin Luther King and Harry Belafonte at the United Nations to publicize their support for the young legislator. But Bond had his detractors as well. The *National Review* noted that Americans should "not doubt the glee with which our enemies are exploiting this dilemma opened by our tolerant ways." Referring to the outcry of support for Bond, the *Review* further noted that there were "no tears for the countrymen dying in Vietnam to preserve the freedom Julian Bond so recklessly abuses."

In an effort to thwart Bond's court case, the state quickly held a special election to fill Bond's seat. If Bond lost the special election, perhaps the case would be mooted—declared irrelevant—by the courts. But Bond received 100 percent of the votes—no one would run against him. Malcolm Dean, his opponent in the original election, had even offered to run Bond's campaign this time around.

In February, a three-man federal court in Atlanta met to consider the case. "The federal court," said Morgan, "simply had to rule that the First, Fourteenth, and Fifteenth amendments forbade penalizing a legislator for his race or speech." The court did just the opposite, upholding the right of Georgia's legislators to refuse to seat Julian Bond. It was a split decision. The majority opinion held that there is nothing in the Georgia constitution to compel the House to seat a member "if a reasonable basis ... exists for the denial." But in his dissent, Chief Justice Elbert P. Tuttle argued that the Georgia House had gone beyond their own constitution in barring Bond without even considering the "grave" question of whether they had violated the guarantee of free speech. Judge Tuttle pointed out that Georgia's charter listed the specific qualifications for a legislator: age, residence requirement, absence of a criminal record. To allow the legislature to bar a member by "undefined, unknown, and even unconstitutionally questionable standards, shocks not only the judicial, but also the lay sense of justice."

With an appeal headed for the Supreme Court, Bond secured the advice of two additional attorneys, including Leonard Boudin of the Emergency Civil Liberties Committee. The ECLC was, in a way, the ACLU's direct competition. It was also the organization that had staunchly defended communists during the Red Scare. Even at this late date there were still those at the ACLU who wished to avoid any cooperation with the ECLC. Mel Wulf, general counsel for the ACLU, told Morgan that he should leave the case entirely in the hands of Boudin; the ACLU would not cooperate with the ECLC.

"The ACLU," said Bond, "withdrew with a blast. A blast at me, a blast at my counsel, a blast suggesting that we were all dupes of some vague conspiracy or that we had fallen under the direction of some sinister Marxist forces." Morgan did not wish to withdraw, but was a bit more sanguine about the pullout. "There are plenty of constitutional cases to go around without trying to corner the market," he said.

Leonard Boudin argued the case *Bond* v. *James "Sloppy" Floyd* before the Supreme Court and in early December 1966, the Court handed down its opinion—a unanimous ruling in favor of Bond, stating that the Georgia House violated Bond's First Amendment guarantee of free speech. In the decision, Chief Justice Earl Warren noted that Bond's words were hardly seditious. He was against fighting—by the Viet Cong and by the United States. The First Amendment guarantees free speech, and "requires that legislators be given the widest latitude to express their views on issues of policy. . . . Legislators have an obligation to take positions on controversial political questions so that their constituents can be fully informed of them and better able to assess their qualifications for office." Had the Supreme Court ruled in favor of the Georgia House, the decision would have given state legislatures enormous power to exclude members. No court, federal or state, had ever before overruled the right of a legislature to judge the qualifications of its own members.

Julian Bond was sworn in as a representative from Georgia's 136th district in January 1967, on the same day that segregationist Governor-elect Lester Maddox took his oath of office. "We'll let Bond have his seat," sniffed one state representative, "but we won't like it, and we'll see to it he gets the silent treatment." Bond did get the silent treatment from some of the legislators. He also got two thousand dollars in back pay and an enormous boost to his political career, much to the chagrin of the old-timers in the South. "Without question," said *Time* magazine, "state legislatures will henceforth hesitate before barring or expelling members without very good cause."

"The ACLU has lobbied for every single piece of civil rights legislation, starting with the 1964 Civil Rights Act," said ACLU president Nadine Strossen. The record bears this out. In Washington, the Union was a vocal supporter of civil rights. But the ACLU, at its core, was dedicated to the preservation of constitutional rights for everyone. Thus, when New York's Mayor John Lindsay denied segregationist Alabama Governor George Wallace the right to use Shea Stadium, a publicly-owned facility, the ACLU supported Wallace. Eleanor Holmes Norton, an assistant legal director from the ACLU, argued the case in the Queens Supreme Court. "I was fresh out of Mississippi," said Norton, "fresh out of marches, and still deeply involved with Fanny Lou Hammer and the Mississippi Freedom Democratic Party." Wallace, on the other hand, was the symbol of southern racism: as Norton put it "the unreconstructed George Wallace."

The ACLU did not inform the Wallace camp that the attorney they were sending was a young African-American. Even so, the men from Alabama didn't flinch when Norton appeared in court to argue successfully for Wallace's right to speak. "I thought it was a magic moment," said Norton, "not only for the ACLU, but for me, a moment that demonstrated how truly I believed in free speech." Norton went on to become Lindsay's city commissioner on human rights. "When I would speak in public," she recalled, "one of the ways I was introduced was 'this is the sister George Wallace needed to get his First Amendment rights.'"

Chapter 11

Free Speech in the Military:
The Howard Levy Case

The first charge was disobeying an order. The second charge was that I had made statements and written a letter to promote disloyalty and disaffection among the army troops. That's a straightforward free speech issue—the only thing I was charged with was saying things and writing things. The third charge was conduct unbecoming an officer and a gentleman—I thought the two were mutually exclusive, but that's another issue.

—Howard Levy

The court-martial of Howard Levy encompassed war crimes, military discipline, Green Berets, freedom of speech, poison ivy, the Hippocratic Oath, the philosophy of Jean-Paul Sartre, and a basic physics lesson: when an unmovable object (the United States Army) meets an irresistible force (Chuck Morgan), something is likely to blow up. It was also a boxing match—in one corner was the army-as-sumo-wrestler-in-fatigues; in the other, Chuck Morgan, trying his darndest to be Muhammad Ali. In the middle of it all stood Howard Levy, a self-described "brash, Jewish, Brooklyn kid who just happened to be a dermatologist." His commanding officer described him as a "pinko"; *Newsweek* called him a "self-seeking martyr." Morgan, for once, kept it simple. "Howard Levy," he said, "was an excellent physician who opposed the Vietnam war."

Howard Brett Levy was commissioned an officer in the United States Army Reserve in 1962. As a medical student, his tour of active duty was deferred until he completed his dermatology training and his residencies at University Hospital, Manhattan Veterans Hospital, and Bellevue in New York. Years later, Levy recalled that he had started out in an apolitical frame of mind, but became increasingly distressed by the poverty he saw in his welfare patients, and by the racism endemic in the health care system. When, in 1963, he joined a picket line of striking welfare workers, he realized that he had become political. And as he neared the end of his residency, he realized that he was profoundly against America's involvement in the Vietnam war.

Howard Levy considered his options—they were few. He could go to prison, he could leave the country, or he could serve. Not being a pacifist (he opposed *this* war, not *every* war), he could not claim conscientious objector status. In July 1965, he decided to serve, and reported to Fort Jackson in Columbia, South Carolina, for duty.

It should be said that the army utterly failed in ushering Levy into the military world. Because the standard six-week basic training course for physicians at Fort Sam Houston was overcrowded, the army decided Levy didn't need any basic training at all. They simply issued him orders, a uniform, and his captain's bars. On his first day at Fort Jackson he was given a six-hour crash course in military practices. He was expected to become a full-fledged captain in the United States Army literally overnight.

It should also be said that, for his part, the newly-inducted Levy did not work too hard at being a soldier. "Howard wasn't very good at saluting," conceded one observer. "His hand came up and sort of landed and came down, but it didn't look very good." Levy himself admitted that he did not take the army too seriously. "I was not well suited for the military," he said. "Everything that people did seemed absolutely ludicrous to me, just so painfully funny. I mean saluting and polishing your shoes and just all of the rigmarole." Levy's behavior ran contrary to that of the typical "officer-and-gentleman." He lived off base, and spent his free time on a voter registration project in Columbia. For a while, he worked on a civil rights newspaper. He refused to join the officers' club, letting it be known that he didn't like tennis, golf, or officers. He had the look of a security risk to some Fort Jackson officials. They opened a surveillance file on him and kept track of his comings and goings.

What Levy took seriously was medicine. He was, by all reports, a good doctor, performing his duties, including his training duties, well. He was assigned to instruct medics who rotated through Fort Jackson in various field medicine techniques. For a while, Levy willingly taught them what he could. "I would tell them what I was doing, try to get them to recognize a few basic skin conditions and treatments."

But in talking to his trainees, Levy realized that these medics were not noncombatants with Red Cross armbands. These were aspiring Green Berets, "aidmen" who would become part of a twelve-man squad and who would take part in routine military operations in Vietnam. "These fellows," he said, "were experts in other disciplines, such as demolitions." They were in fact, special forces soldiers, being trained to "develop, organize, equip, and direct indigenous forces in the conduct of guerrilla warfare and to advise, train, and assist host country forces in counterinsurgency operations."

Traditionally, the military had kept the fighting and healing parts of the military separate. With these aidmen, however, the army had created a hybrid: a killer-healer. "I thought that was an illegitimate use of medicine, of medical training. And at that point I drew the line and said I can't do that." Levy refused to train any special forces men. The hospital commander, Colonel Henry F. Fancy, gave him the chance to change his mind. Levy refused. The special forces men "were, in fact, killers," he insisted. "They made no bones of the fact that they did kill peasants and women and children. I didn't make up the rhetoric, they told me."

At first Colonel Fancy planned to issue some sort of mild punishment for Levy, perhaps an administrative reprimand. "I had less than six months to go in the military," said Levy. "Given that fact, I thought they would be wise enough to say, 'Well, let's find some other way to train these Green Beret fellows, let's not make an issue of this, it'll blow up in our faces. Let's get rid of this son-of-a-bitch Levy in six months and we'll be done with it.' That's what my rational side said they would do. The problem is that the military isn't rational." Intelligence officers at the base convinced Colonel Fancy that Levy was a dangerous man. When the colonel reviewed the security file, he agreed. Howard Levy, said Colonel Fancy, was "a pinko." The reprimand became a court-martial.

The first charge filed against Howard Levy was "disobeying an order." Had the army stopped there, Levy would be a footnote in the annals of military justice. But the army elected to charge him with other crimes: with attempting to promote "disloyalty and disaffection among the troops" and with "making intemperate, defamatory, provoking, and disloyal statements" to special forces personnel while in uniform. He was accused of having said, "The United States is wrong in being involved in the Vietnam War. I would refuse to go to Vietnam if ordered to do so."

To these charges, the army later added still more: "conduct unbecoming an officer and a gentleman" and writing a letter that interfered with "loyalty, morale, and discipline." And, indeed, Levy had written a letter to an Army Sergeant Geoffrey Hancock Jr., then serving in Vietnam. In the letter, Levy wrote, "Geoffrey, who are you fighting for? Do you know? Have you thought about it? Your real battle is back here in the U.S., but why must I fight it for you?" Just a few short months from an honorable discharge, Levy found himself facing a prison term of eleven years. "I needed a lawyer," he said. "So I called Chuck Morgan of the ACLU, and I became an ACLU case."

Chuck Morgan's initial assessment of the Levy case was dismay, rendered in typical Morgan style. "Why, the way you would have read the army's charges against him you would have thought that he had stood up on the back of a truck and spoken to the entire mass of the American armed services," he said. But Morgan did admit that Levy's anti-war statements were strong stuff. "When he said special forces men are killers of women and children and murderers of peasants," he said, "that probably bothered them."

The central legal issue for the ACLU was free speech: Does the Bill of Rights apply to the military? Can a soldier speak openly about his views? Does this right change if the soldier is in uniform? Does the right change if the soldier is in a combat zone? Even within the ACLU, the answers were not entirely clear. "There were all these institutions," said Ira Glasser, "enclave institutions—mental hospitals, prisons, foster care institutions, the military, public schools, even—where the Constitution had never penetrated. The people who ran those institutions took the position that the Bill of Rights didn't apply to them. If you distributed a leaflet out on the street, a cop couldn't arrest you for it, but if you tried it in the army, you could get court-martialed."

In a way, the Levy case was ideal for the ACLU—a First

Amendment case that could conceivably push the frontier of free speech. But the case, with its anti-war overtones, was a very political one. Some ACLU folks in the New York office were worried about the kind of publicity Levy's case could attract. Levy's statements made for great copy. He compared Lyndon Johnson to Adolf Hitler and the Green Berets to Nazi Storm troopers, and he had suggested that the real battle for freedom was at home. Morgan, too, made for great copy: "At the drop of a hint," wrote one reporter, "he will pour another round of drinks, stoke another of his big, self-consciously Churchillian cigars, and talk deep into the night with a racehorse logic that leaves listeners gasping for breath."

The army was equally worried about political fallout from the case. Levy was Jewish and the last thing they wanted was the appearance of a Dreyfus case, in which a French-Jewish army officer was arrested for spying in 1894, then sentenced to life imprisonment on Devil's Island. Soon after the trial, documents that proved his innocence were turned over to the authorities, but the French army was so bitterly anti-Semitic that this new evidence was quashed. It took another ten years to secure Dreyfus's release. Amazingly, Dreyfus returned to the army, earned the rank of major, and was enrolled in the Legion of Honor. But his name became synonymous with scapegoating in the military. During the Levy case, the Dreyfus affair was mentioned time and again. In an effort to avoid any appearance of anti-Semitism, the U.S. Army brought in a Jewish prosecutor, reasoning that the presence of a Jewish officer on the other side of the case would bring an appearance of fairness to the whole proceeding. But anti-Semitism tinged the case throughout. Both sides received anti-Semitic mail, and one local newspaper, claiming that Levy was supported by Jewish-dominated groups from New York, wondered "if they would likewise admire a refusal to cooperate with our government's war if U.S. forces were dispatched to Israel instead of Vietnam." "Throughout the trial," wrote Nicholas Von Hoffman, "you got the feeling the captain might have done better if he hadn't been Jewish and something of a pop-off with a splendidly meddlesome manner."

Before the court-martial began, Morgan went before the federal court in Washington, D.C., to stop the proceedings. The U.S. Military Court of Appeals had recently ruled that the Miranda decision guaranteeing counsel and other procedural safeguards applied to the armed forces. Shouldn't free speech apply as well? The three-judge panel refused to block the court-martial, but they did agree that the charges were vague, ill-defined, and possibly unconstitutional. This added to the army judicial staff's worries. The army chose one of their most-respected judges—Colonel Earl V. Brown of Washington, D.C.—to hear the case. He, along with the ten-officer panel who served during the court-martial, realized that the case would likely receive judicial scrutiny down the road.

The facts of the case were not contested. Levy freely admitted to disobeying the order, and admitted that he had said and written things critical of the war. Morgan and the rest of the ACLU legal team pulled together as broad a defense as they could, arguing for constitutional and professional considerations that supported Levy in his refusal to train the Green Berets. "Levy," said Burt Neuborne, "was one of the first cases where we locked onto the individual and said that the only way that we can really provide effective representation for these ideas is to represent the person and raise every possible defense we could."

Before the trial had even started, the whole thing took on some of the carnival aspects that had dominated the Scopes trial fifty years earlier. Reporters from all over the country came to cover the case, and the motels and diners around Fort Jackson filled quickly with the media and the ACLU legal entourage. Morgan camped out for weeks in one motel room, holding court late into the night for the defense team and the press. Ira Glasser remembers coming into town at midnight to find fifty people in Morgan's room. "Morgan was lying in bed, giving orders. There was a jug of bourbon there on the floor next to him."

To some, Morgan was reminiscent of Clarence Darrow; to others he was more Cecil B. DeMille. "He was the producer," said Norman Siegel. "His room was filled with very talented, creative, and energetic people who were committed to that case. Chuck was moving them in and out, giving them orders. He had people in that room who were not even friendly with each other, but he figured out how to make them into a team." Even Fort Jackson itself took on a little of the excitement. "We would walk down the street of Fort Jackson on the way to the courtroom," recalled Levy, "and GIs would hang out of their windows and their barracks to give us the "V" sign, to raise the clenched fist, and to cheer us on." Captain Levy took to showing up at the courtroom with his brass unpolished and his shirt collar open. He had given up saluting altogether, and instead waved at the MPs standing guard at the courtroom steps.

But in fact, the real carnival took place inside the courtroom, out of public view. During the trial Morgan called army physicians who testified that they would also refuse to train Green Berets, giving professional reasons. Why should a trained soldier be given the job of using dangerous drugs? Why should medical judgment be subordinated to military judgment? He called character witnesses to vouch for Levy's patriotism. Levy's father, who took the stand holding a Bible and a small American flag that had been in his son's room since childhood, testified. "I know my son. He follows his convictions, and he has the guts to do it."

The army called witnesses to vouch for its practice of training special service men. One said that "if I were a Viet Cong...I'd rather have a Green Beret shoot me than someone untrained because it's logical to assume that if he didn't kill me, in a few min-

utes he would help me." On cross-examination, Morgan got
Colonel Fancy to testify that he had originally planned a mild
punishment for Levy but had changed his mind when he saw
Levy's security file. Morgan asked in pre-trial hearings and during the trial to see the file but his requests were denied. It was
classified, and Morgan had no security clearance. Morgan asked
if Levy's army-appointed lawyer could read the file, and the
court agreed, but only if the lawyer did not divulge the contents
to anyone. Morgan had to conduct a defense without ever
knowing the contents of the file that had triggered the court-
martial in the first place.

Taking a cue from the federal court judges, Morgan set out to
prove that some of the charges were vague and ill-defined:

> Morgan: "He [Levy] never made you disloyal, did he?"
> Witness: "No."
> Morgan: "He never made you disaffect, did he?"
> Witness: "What does 'disaffect' mean?"
> Morgan: "I don't know."
> Colonel Brown: "Mr. Morgan, if you don't know the questions,
> don't ask 'em."
> Morgan: "I don't know the meaning of the word 'disaffection.'"
> Brown: "Well, do not use it in a question, then."
> Morgan: "May I have instructions from the Court then as to
> the meaning of the word?"
> Brown: "You should have asked for it before you asked the
> question."
> Morgan: "I asked for a ruling... the other day."
> Brown: "You should have asked me some time ago."
> Morgan: "I asked you... the other day."
> Brown: "It's not a proper legal proceeding to pose questions
> and then come back with a quick retort that you don't know the
> meaning of the words you used in your question."

Morgan: "The witness said he didn't know. . . . Colonel, I'm trying to get from you . . . the legal definition of disaffection."

Brown: "You don't need it at this time . . . I told you I'd give you
the legal definition . . . at the end of the trial."

Morgan: "If I don't know the definition I don't know how to
proceed."

The press began to make jokes about Major Confusion and
General Psychosis. Morgan told reporters that he kept a copy of
Kafka's *The Trial* in his hotel room as a reference book.

The court-martial was not going well for Levy. The panel of
ten officers—nine of whom wore the combat infantryman's
badge, four of whom had served in Vietnam—showed little com-
passion for this anti-war doctor and his outspoken defense lawyer.
But then, halfway through the proceedings, Colonel Brown suggested that he would be willing to consider an unusual defense:
the war crime doctrine of Nuremberg. "My research," Brown said,
"discloses the Nuremberg trials involve a rule that a soldier must
refuse an order to commit a war crime." Perhaps a doctor would
not be "morally bound" to train Green Berets if they were war
criminals? If it could be shown that by obeying the order Levy was
helping the special forces men commit war crimes, Brown said,
the major charge against him would be dropped.

Morgan was stunned: in case after case, those who refused to
fight in Vietnam had tried to contend that the U.S. was com-
mitting war crimes. In case after case, the right to present that
defense had been rejected. Now an army colonel was suggesting
that Morgan use war crimes as a defense strategy. "When war
crimes were mentioned at the trial," said Levy, "I was absolutely
flabbergasted." Morgan's response was pragmatic: "I'll need an
extra day to prove war crimes," he said, and he set out to do it.
"There were a lot of people in the ACLU who were very nervous
about the war crimes defense," said Ira Glasser. "They knew that

free speech was a civil liberties issue—but why should we be involved with war crimes issues? That was too political."

Morgan had no time for the faint-hearted at the ACLU. "My job was to defend that client," he said. "That's what I got a law license for. And it was to raise every question in that client's defense and carry him all the way and win if possible." So, while there was a fair amount of joking in the defense strategy sessions—various ACLU operatives threatened to call in the Viet Cong or subpoena the Chinese government for war crimes information—there was fevered research going on as well. Morgan sent out a public call for evidence of war crimes. The response was overwhelming: a telegram from Jean-Paul Sartre; a crate of documents from Bertrand Russell's office; four thousand newspaper clippings from a Columbia University professor. In the San Francisco area, 121 medical students signed petitions declaring they would refuse to serve with the armed forces in Vietnam if drafted. One hundred faculty members at Stanford and the University of California Medical Center signed petitions in support. The war crimes aspect of the case only intensified media interest. "The American press," said Morgan, "had come upon the only war crimes trial in the United States' continental history."

In six days time, Morgan presented Colonel Brown a new brief and three new defense witnesses. Donald Duncan, a former Green Beret then at *Ramparts* magazine, testified that special forces men paid a bounty of ten dollars for the right ear of each enemy brought in by the Vietnamese forces, and that the U.S. aidmen routinely stood by when South Vietnamese forces tortured prisoners. Captain Peter Borne testified that a bound prisoner was left to burn to death in a village by South Vietnamese forces and that when he complained, his commanding officer said, "Don't rock the boat." He told the military panel that "beatings, brutality were the order of the day. When it started, we would turn around and light a cigarette." Author Robin Moore,

who wrote the bestseller *Green Beret*, said U.S. troops were help-
less to prevent South Vietnamese atrocities, and that aidmen
used their medical training to administer sodium pentothal, the
so-called truth serum, to captured Viet Cong.

Observers felt there was at least enough evidence to demonstrate American complicity in war crimes, but Colonel Brown
wanted more. He wanted proof of a pattern of complicity; Morgan, he said, had only brought in isolated incidents. Morgan argued that enough isolated incidents constitute a pattern, but
Brown ruled that "while there have been perhaps instances of
needless brutality in the struggle in Vietnam...there is no evidence that would render this order to train aidmen illegal on
the grounds that eventually these men would become engaged
in war crimes or in some way prostitute their medical training
by employing it in crimes against humanity." The war crimes
defense was denied.

In a way, Morgan was relieved. "At last," he said, "I can get
back to the business of defending my client instead of prosecuting the whole damn army." But when the war crimes defense
evaporated, so did any chance for Levy's acquittal. Morgan succeeded in having the letter-writing charge dropped, but the
panel found Levy guilty on all other counts. He was sentenced
to three years hard labor.

"As soon as the verdict was read," recalled Levy, "there was
screaming and wailing in the courtroom, my mother was crying,
my girlfriend was crying. Pandemonium broke out. And then
within minutes after the verdict was rendered, I was grabbed by
two burly military police, who put my arms behind my back and
clapped handcuffs on me. The next thing I knew I was being literally shoved down the aisle of the courtroom, out the front
door, into an MP car, and driven off to a locked cell. As I looked
behind, I saw Chuck Morgan running down the street of this
army base after the car. Chuck at that point weighed about

three hundred pounds. But there was Chuck just waving his hands and screaming and yelling and running after this military police car. They left him in the dust."

Morgan registered a strong complaint against this rough handling of his client, and so did the Pentagon. Army top brass were not pleased to see the televised picture of one of their officers being hauled about in handcuffs like a common criminal. Levy was removed from the locked cell, and for lack of better facilities was held in a hospital ward at Fort Jackson while the base commander reviewed the case. Morgan filed nine separate military and civil petitions for Levy's release pending appeal, but lost in each case. One officer testified that he had received information from a "confidential source" which revealed Levy's intention to flee to a communist country. Levy spent two years in the Fort Leavenworth Military Prison, then several months in a federal penitentiary, before he was finally released by order of Supreme Court Justice William O. Douglas in August 1969. But in 1974, the Supreme Court upheld the Levy conviction. "The Supreme Court," noted Norman Siegel, "said that in the military you don't have the same First Amendment rights that you have as a citizen."

Years later, Chuck Morgan pondered the Levy case again. "Now, did we win anything? Well, I think so. Did people of the United States gain a greater understanding of the Vietnam war? Sure. Did the ACLU itself gain a greater understanding of the Vietnam war? Sure." But not all of the ACLU welcomed the lessons of the Levy case. "There was some sniper fire," Morgan admitted. "Some of the ACLU liberals were angry at my war crimes defense." Some members of the board saw Morgan's activities as a political assault on the war, and not a civil liberties case. Politics, of course, was anathema to the ACLU—as was

Morgan himself, to some. When Morgan went to the hospital after a fall, a telegram arrived from New York: "The ACLU executive committee," Morgan relates, "wished me a speedy recovery—four-to-two, with five abstentions."

Baldwin, "the mixture of opposite parts." *(Sophia Smith Collection, Smith College)*

An illustration of what has been called the ACLU's "poisonous even-handedness" in its choice of clients. Opposite: the Scottsboro case, in which nine young African-Americans were unfairly convicted of rape in the segregationist South, 1932. Top, the defendents leaving the courthouse; bottom, one of the defendents on trial. The ACLU took on the case for the U.S. Supreme Court appeal. *(The ACLU of Southern California)* Below: at the same time, the ACLU took on cases defending the KKK's rights to free speech and assembly. Here the Klan parade in Springfield, Ohio, in 1923. *(Library of Congress)*

Morris Ernst (book in hand) during the Customs Court *Ulysses* case. (*Harry Ransom Humanities Research Center, University of Texas*)

Workers Alliance March in Washington, D.C., 1930s. *(National Archives)*

A lifetime of activism—
Elizabeth Gurley Flynn
in her late teens, 1908.
(*Library of Congress*)

Elizabeth Gurley Flynn during an arrest
while organizing mine workers in Minnesota, 1916. (*Library of Congress*)

Elizabeth Gurley Flynn after her expulsion from the ACLU in 1940.
(*Library of Congress*)

Roger Baldwin in the mid-1930s with Madeline Doty at left, reading an anti-fascist publication of the American League Against War and Fascism. (*Mudd Library, Princeton University*)

ACLU attorney Morris Ernst in 1939, one of the several ACLU leaders growing increasingly uncomfortable with the Communist Party in America. (*Harry Ransom Humanities Research Center, University of Texas*)

Left to right, George, Hisa, and Yasbie Hirano, relocated from California to the Colorado River Relocation Center in Poston, Arizona, 1942. *(National Archives)*

A young evacuee of Japanese ancestry waits with the the family baggage before leaving by bus for a relocation center, San Francisco, California, April, 1942. *(National Archives)*

Two faces of anti-communism in the 1950s. Opposite: Morris Ernst of the ACLU, 1958, who maintained a secret correspondence with FBI officials (*Harry Ransom Humanities Research Center, University of Texas*); below: Senator Joseph McCarthy, whose wayward accusations ended careers and ruined lives in the early years of the decade. (*National Archives*)

Chuck Morgan of the ACLU in Washington, D.C., 1970. (*Charles Morgan Jr.*)

Representative Julian Bond of Georgia, 1968. (*National Archives*)

Col. Vernon V. Brown, presiding officer at the court-martial of Captain Howard Levy, entering the courtroom at Fort Jackson, South Carolina, 1967. *(State Record Newspapers, Columbia, South Carolina)*

Members of the court-martial panel leaving the courtroom during a recess in the proceedings. *(State Record Newspapers, Columbia, South Carolina)*

Attorney Morgan
quizzing an M.P.
*(State Record Newspa-
pers, Columbia, South
Carolina)*

Captain Howard Levy
leaving the courtroom
in handcuffs after the
verdict was announced.
(Dr. Howard Levy)

Captain Howard Levy attending his own court-martial. (*Dr. Howard Levy*)

Above and below: The "explosion of rights" in the early 1970s. The ACLU marching for free speech on campus, and for the United Farm Workers. (*The ACLU of Southern California*)

Protesting school segregation in California. (*The ACLU of Southern California*)

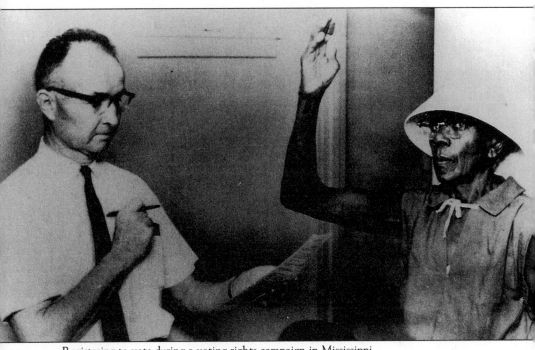

Registering to vote during a voting rights campaign in Mississippi.
(*The ACLU of Southern California*)

Baldwin, in his supposed retirement—above: at work in his New York office; opposite: Baldwin addressing an ACLU rally in Southern California. (*The National Office of the ACLU*)

Protesting the ACLU's impeachment campaign in California. (*The ACLU of Southern California*)

Chapter 12

High Crimes
and Hate Speech:
From Watergate to Skokie

*When the Nazis march, they're expressing bigotry. We in
the ACLU despise their bigotry, but we will defend their right
to march when it's being denied. The First Amendment pro-
tects the expression of bigotry.*

—*Sarah Wunsch*

Chuck Morgan moved to the ACLU's Washington, D.C., office in 1972 and made the place his bully pulpit. He
preached the gospel of activism to the entire ACLU, and kept
a sharp eye on the goings-on across town at the White House.
Before the year was out, he was going after President Richard
Nixon. "Chuck Morgan saw civil liberties issues where nobody
else saw them, and before anybody else saw them," said Ira
Glasser, who directed the New York affiliate in the 1970s. "He
called me up one day, and said that we should call for the impeachment of Richard Nixon because of his persistent violation
of civil liberties. It was sort of like telling me that dinosaurs
were walking the earth again—impeachment was something
that just didn't happen."

"I remember first hearing Chuck going after Nixon," said Jay

Miller, "and I said, 'Chuck has gone crazy.'" And in the early months of the Watergate scandal, many others agreed. The whole thing looked like nothing more than a botched burglary attempt on the part of a few Republican crackpots. There was no real evidence tying the president to the burglary and the ensuing cover-up, but Morgan was emphatic. "Richard Nixon was masterminding a campaign to deprive people of their liberties all across the country," he said later. "We had wiretaps of the opposing party's political processes, we had prosecutions of people dissenting against the war. Richard Nixon unloosed all sorts of spy groups in the United States and through the Justice Department and the government."

Around the country, Morgan did have some supporters within the Union. As early as 1971, the Southern California office had called for Nixon's impeachment for his role in the Vietnam war. Once the Watergate break-in occurred, other affiliates chimed in. Morgan was spearheading a campaign that made the national office nervous. "The impeachment forum," said Norman Dorsen, ACLU president in the 1970s, "was very different from the other forums in which the ACLU was active, namely the courts or Congress. Impeachment had a heavy political element in it."

One of the ACLU's bedrock principles had been political non-partisanship. The call for impeachment would give the ACLU the appearance of being pro-Democrat, anti-Nixon, or both. "This would hurt the ACLU in the long run," said Dorsen. Morgan himself admitted that there was an undeniable air of partisanship surrounding the Watergate case, partly because he was an undeniably partisan man. "Was I a Democrat? Sure," he admitted later. "Was I a loyal member of the Alabama Democratic Party? You bet your bippy. Had I ever voted for a Republican in my life? I can't recall having ever done so. But Richard Nixon brought the massive power of the presidency down against individuals who disagreed with him. He himself became an enemy of the people, and the Constitution provides remedies for that."

The ACLU national board officially took up the issue in September 1973, in a debate that went on for six hours. By this time, impeachment was by no means a dinosaur—it had been openly discussed in Congress. Still, the ACLU knew it had to carefully consider its position. "We were concerned," said Burt Neuborne, "about irrevocably politicizing ourselves. In other words, would we be forever perceived as an arm of the Democratic party?" At the meeting, law professor Monroe Freeman argued that "we should not express our individual feelings through the institution of the ACLU," and several speakers said the Union should take no action whatsoever on impeachment. But Morgan spoke last. He stood firmly for impeachment, and in folksy fashion lectured the assembled board. Presidents are teachers, he said. Truman taught the nation to love the piano, Eisenhower taught Americans to love golf. Nixon was teaching the country to lie and to degrade the Constitution. The applause for his words was thunderous, and the vote went fifty-one to five in favor of calling for Richard Nixon's impeachment. The ACLU was the first organization in the country to take such a stand.

A few of the more timid souls at the Union hoped that they could be circumspect in their newly-adopted position, but the current director, Aryeh Neier, working with Morgan, Dorsen, and Ira Glasser, moved quickly to take the position to the people. Two weeks after the vote, the Union bought full page ads in several major newspapers, including *The New York Times*. "WHY IT IS NECESSARY TO IMPEACH PRESIDENT NIXON AND HOW IT CAN BE DONE," ran the block letter headline. The ad explained the Union's reasons for taking so strong a stand on impeachment, and set out the constitutional issues at stake. "President Nixon," read the ad, "means to function above the law. If he is allowed to continue, then the destruction of the Bill of Rights could follow." The text went on to list President Nixon's offenses: he had approved political surveillance and established a secret police force to spy on the private lives of those who opposed him. He had authorized illegal bombing in Cambodia, and had approved of thirteen thousand illegal arrests made in Washington, D.C., in May 1971. The president's campaign was an "engineering of restraint," one that limited the freedom of the press and used the grand jury system and the Internal Revenue Service as harassment tools.

The strongly-worded ad featured a small clip-out coupon at the bottom of the page, inviting the reader to join the campaign for impeachment by joining the ACLU. Annual dues for individuals ran fifteen dollars a year. Twenty-five thousand new members came on board. "Nixon was wildly unpopular," said Burt Neuborne. "The ACLU was perceived as finally being on the side of the majority, which made some of us nervous. I mean I get very nervous when I'm on the side of the majority." Not to worry; the Nixon impeachment call made the ACLU popular, but only for the moment.

In the summer of 1976, the National Socialist Party of America was a familiar feature in Marquette Park on the south side of Chicago—a dozen or so men parading in Nazi uniforms. The demonstrations, slipshod and occasionally raucous, attracted a few supporters from the community. They also attracted counter-demonstrators, offended by the NSPA's rank racism and by its call for the forced deportation of all Jews and blacks from America. During one demonstration, violence erupted between the NSPA and the Martin Luther King Jr. Coalition. The Chicago Park District, hoping to avoid further trouble, put a stop to all demonstrations by enforcing an old and little-used ordinance requiring $250,000 in liability insurance from any group wanting to hold a public demonstration in a Chicago park.

Frank Collin, head of the NSPA, promptly turned to the ACLU for help. The ACLU filed a suit on his behalf, charging that the ordinance essentially restricted free speech for the NSPA and for any other group that would wish to use the public space. The suit, filed in district court, was likely to drag on for a year or more, and Collin, unwilling to wait, decided to find another spot for his parades. He sent out about a dozen requests for march permits to several Chicago-area communities on an NSPA letterhead that featured a swastika. Most local governments simply ignored him, but the village of Skokie, just north of Chicago, informed him that he would need a $350,000 insurance bond to parade in their village. Collin wrote back to inform them that he intended to stage a peaceful protest of the insurance bond requirement on the steps of the Skokie village hall on May 1, 1977.

"It's not that we begin each day by saying, 'Which clients shall we take today to stir up some controversy,'" said Alan Reitman of the ACLU. "We don't create our clients; in my view, history creates them." If so, the history that went into the making of Frank Collin was pathetic indeed. In his mid-thirties, grandiose, prevaricating, Collin was by any measure a disturbed man. He copied Hitler's hairstyle, wore jackboots, and used a bullhorn to trumpet his plans for "an all-white America" at his ragtag rallies in Marquette Park. He had once belonged to George Lincoln Rockwell's American Nazi Party. But when the Nazis got wind of a report stating that Collin's real name was Cohn, and that his father was Jewish, they kicked him out. Collin vehemently denied the report, and left the Party an embittered man. Rockwell was assassinated in 1967 by one of his own followers. When Collin founded the NSPA, he hoped to become the new leader of Nazism in America.

Unlike the German American Bund of the 1930s, which once turned out a crowd of several thousand in New York City to celebrate Hitler's birthday, the NSPA rarely attracted more than a few dozen followers to any event. But Collin was wise in the ways of publicity—he knew that any headline at all would help his cause. He also knew that a proposed march in Skokie would get him headlines, because Skokie was no ordinary town. Half of its seventy thousand residents were Jewish and about one thousand were Holocaust survivors.

At first, Skokie officials planned to let the NSPA demonstration take place. They hoped the Nazis would stage their protest and then disappear. The mayor informed community leaders, including leaders in the community's seven synagogues, about the impending protest, and urged restraint and caution on the part of all. The community response was immediate, and impassioned. "We don't want to wake up on May 2 and find that nothing was done," one Holocaust survivor told the mayor. "We are a special breed of people, we went through unbelievable things. History doesn't even know the things that happened to us.... I appeal to you once more. This thing should not happen in our village." The residents were joined by groups from outside Skokie, who let the town know they planned to come in during the march to stage a huge counter-demonstration. Facing the prospect of serious violence, the mayor changed his mind, banned the demonstration, and filed suit to stop any public display by the NSPA in Skokie.

One could say that Skokie played right into Collin's hand. He would have been hard-pressed to turn out more than twenty people in uniform, but with the ban and the lawsuit, newspapers across Chicago ran stories on the squelched "Nazi rally," making the NSPA appear larger and far more threatening than it could ever be. But there were residents of Skokie who could not countenance any Nazi presence in their town and their outcry was simply too passionate to ignore. "We were accused that we went like sheep," said one man, speaking of the Holocaust. "At that time we were hunted by everybody, not just by Nazis, but hunted by every human being.... But now we must be strong and not silent." Roger Baldwin, then in his nineties, suc-cinctly pegged the unfolding crisis when he said, "Skokie is a very conspicuous confrontation between the Nazis and the people they hurt the most."

Frank Collin was just one of a group of clients the Chicago ACLU handled in 1977. According to one staffer, they repre-sented dozens of clients ranging from politicians to prostitutes to "Jews for Jesus" to a group of high school students who wanted the right to watch violent movies. It was a busy year, but not an usual one, until April 27, when Collin brought his case against Skokie to David Goldberger, legal director of the Chicago ACLU, and asked, yet again, for help. "It was the kind of case, Goldberger said later, "that made me think, 'Gee, can I find a volunteer attorney to do this one?'"

The Chicago ACLU, like most affiliates, routinely used vol-unteer lawyers for their cases, and Goldberger tried, without success, to find one. Every single lawyer he called was either unwilling or unable to take on Collin's case. Goldberger had no choice but to take it on himself. "I despised Collin's views," he said, "and he despised me, because I'm a Jew." But Goldberger was also a deeply committed lawyer who had worked almost ex-clusively for the ACLU since he had graduated from the Chicago University School of Law. "There is a well-established American historical tradition that supports the representation of unpopular clients," he later wrote, noting that John Adams had defended a British soldier charged with killing colonists during the Boston Massacre and Roger Taney represented an abolitionist in the slave state of Maryland. "I deeply believe," Goldberger wrote, "that every attorney has an ethical obligation to represent unpopular clients."

Within a day, Goldberger, Collin, and the Skokie attorney went before Chancery Judge Joseph Wosik to present their respective arguments. "The case is a classic First Amendment case, Your Honor," said Goldberger. "It tests the very foundation of democracy. The village of Skokie moves for an order enjoining speech before it has occurred, even though that speech is to occur in an orderly fashion in front of the village hall for a period of between twenty and thirty minutes on a Sunday afternoon." The village of Skokie argued that community reaction to the demonstration would likely be violent; there could be great harm done to individuals and to the community as a whole, and therefore the demonstration should be banned. Judge Wosik agreed, and ruled that an injunction should be issued to stop the May 1 demonstration. A day later, the Illinois appeals court upheld Judge Wosik's decision.

Collin, shrewdly noting that the injunction specified no demonstration on May 1, announced plans to demonstrate on April 30, instead. Skokie immediately went back to court and won an injunction against all Nazi demonstrations, and in the following days, passed several ordinances aimed at stopping the Nazis entirely. One ordinance made illegal any public display of "symbols offensive to the community"—such as the swastika. "The village of Skokie," said one ACLU staffer, "has shredded the First Amendment."

The case was widely reported in the papers, on radio, and on television around Chicago. Almost immediately, the Chicago ACLU began receiving hundreds of calls. Some people demanded that Goldberger be removed from the case because he was Jewish, but most demanded that the ACLU drop the case altogether. The interest in the case grew rapidly, and Goldberger was asked to speak at several forums about the ACLU's defense of the Nazis. Everywhere he went, he encountered angry demonstrators. At one speaking engagement a group tried to put a rope around his neck, calling it "an award." At another, hecklers accused him of being no better than the Jews that helped the Nazis in the death camps. When he appeared on the "Donahue" show, he was told there would be a few people in the audience from the other side. In fact, the show's producers packed the studio with people who had survived the concentration camps. "Would you, the ACLU, defend the Nazis in Germany? If not, why do you defend them now?" asked one man in the audience. "Do you know what will happen if this ideology, if these ideas come to the power? Do you know who'll be shot? Mr. Goldberger, you. You'll be the first one." The man then rolled up his sleeve, and showed Phil Donahue the tattoo he had gotten in the concentration camp. "They led the questioning," Goldberger recalled. "It was the most intense experience I ever went through in my life."

People across the country were outraged at the ACLU. The Jewish Defense League picketed ACLU offices in New York, California, and Florida. In New York, they presented ACLU director Aryeh Neier with an engraved brass plaque: "Presented to the ACLU on Hitler's Birthday." When David Goldberger spoke at the ACLU's Convocation on Free Speech in New York that summer, he found many in the crowd hostile to him personally. "This way to Auschwitz," called out one bystander as Goldberger walked into the room. During the question period, one woman asked if Goldberger would defend the Nazis if they wanted to march down a street in his neighborhood. "Lady," he replied, "defending them *is* like having them march in my neighborhood."

The ACLU had its supporters, of course. One writer in the *Nation* pointed out that "political debate—'uninhibited, robust, and wide open,' in parks and streets as well as lecture halls—will rouse anger and give offense. Public offensiveness, like private

distress, is an unavoidable cost of freedom." In the years following Skokie, the debate continued. "When you hear about the
ACLU defending these horrific people, you react with revul-
sion," conceded Julian Bond. "The Klan, Nazis, who knows what.
Awful, awful people. But then you think about it, and you say, 'Is
this the right of the Nazis to march in Skokie or is this the right
of unpopular people to march in an area where they're terrifically
unpopular?' And if you look at it that way then you have to stand
with the ACLU." Even the staunchest supporters of community
rights agreed that Skokie went too far in 1977. "Ultimately," said
Roger Conner of the Center for Community Interest, "a community doesn't have a right to insulate itself against an idea that
it finds disagreeable. Not in our country."

Some defended the ACLU for philosophical reasons. "When
we allow false and vicious speech, it identifies itself," said
Anthony Lewis. "It defines itself, and it lets us know who the bad
guys are. To tolerate such speech is the symbol of a self-confident
society." But there are critics who feel that when words are likely
to result in violent deeds, society must suppress speech. "The
Nazis," said William Donohue, "are not just an unpopular group.
They are urban terrorists. There is a danger in treating them as if
they were the Boy Scouts. These are people who have an agenda
to subvert the meaning of the First Amendment and they have
unwitting accomplices in the American Civil Liberties Union."

The Illinois Supreme Court refused to put the ACLU's appeal
on the fast track; they essentially told Goldberger that Collin
would have to wait his turn. Realizing that this could take
months, Goldberger sent U.S. Supreme Court Justice John Paul
Stevens a petition asking for immediate help. Justice Stevens
presented it to the full Court, and on June 14 it ruled that any
citizen subject to prior restraint of speech was entitled to be

heard in court quickly, or to have the restraint removed. Collin, knowing the state now had an obligation of swift review, announced his intention to demonstrate in Skokie on July 4. The Illinois Court of Appeals scheduled the hearing for July 6. At the appeal, the Skokie lawyers argued that the demonstration would end in violence and should be stopped. They also argued that the swastika constituted "fighting words," a form of speech not protected under the First Amendment, and as such should be banned, even if the NSPA was allowed to demonstrate. But "fighting words" is a legal doctrine that generally applies to one-on-one confrontations and comes into play after the words are spoken, not before. The appeals court sent the case back to the lower court for further review.

Goldberger's "classic First Amendment case" jumped from one venue to the next without any final resolution. Meanwhile, the ACLU continued to feel the public's rage. Membership declined across the country, and some at the ACLU blamed Skokie entirely. But membership had begun declining well before the Skokie case hit the newspapers. In 1974, immediately after the Nixon resignation, the membership count stood at 270,000; in 1977, it was at 210,000; in 1978 it dove to 185,000. Skokie accounted for much of this last decline, but before that the drop in numbers could be attributed to a breakup in the liberal East Coast community that made up a large part of the ACLU membership. It was a community that stood solidly together on civil rights, Vietnam, and Watergate, but other issues, particularly those closer to home, split them down the middle. East Coast liberals loudly supported the idea of civil rights in Selma, Alabama, but when desegregation came to Boston, many of the same liberals protested. The emerging women's movement was favored in the abstract, but when white men couldn't get into law school because of affirmative action, they began to protest, too. Liberal politics became fractured, and political groups, including the ACLU, felt it on their membership rolls and in their pocketbooks.

Another reason for the decline in membership goes to the heart of the ACLU's purpose—the Bill of Rights. People rarely joined the Union because they loved these constitutional amendments. They joined because they wanted to support Julian Bond or Howard Levy, or because they wanted Richard Nixon impeached. They left the ACLU not because they disavowed the Bill of Rights, but because they hated Nazis. "The audience for defending the Bill of Rights in the United States will never be very large or diverse," said Julian Bond. "For most of us, the humdrum affairs of daily life, the job, the home, the family, are the paramount issues. The abstract notion of whether or not Nazis can march in Skokie seems so far removed from everyday experience."

Finally, the ACLU's decline in the late 1970s could be blamed on its own history. In 1977, *The New York Times* printed an article headlined "FBI Files Disclose '50s Tie to ACLU." The documents, which the ACLU had gotten under the Freedom of Information Act and then shared with *The Times*, confirmed the worst of the stories about what had gone on in the ACLU in the 1950s. Morris Ernst had snitched on ACLU members with anti-FBI leanings; Patrick Malin had asked the FBI to help him "keep communists off the board of directors"; Herbert Levy, an ACLU lawyer in the 1950s, had asked the FBI's help in sniffing out reputed communists on the ACLU affiliate board in Maryland. Levy, the only one of the three still alive, said he did not remember such communication, and that he never gave the Bureau information that could be used against anyone. But that same summer, when Neier went to Brooklyn Law School as one of two speakers in a debate on Skokie, the other speaker, Marshall Perlin of the National Lawyers Guild, proclaimed that "the ACLU is not as neutral as it pretends. The ACLU did not defend the rights of communists in the 1950s. Why should it be defending people like the Nazis and the Klan today?" Neier fired back, "We were wrong in the fifties. But our failure then shouldn't be invoked as an excuse for comparable failures today." To his credit, Neier openly called all ACLU dealing with the FBI "inexcusable and destructive of civil liberties principles." But this was bad press nonetheless, and coming right in the middle of the Skokie conflict it did the organization little good. And the Union, in its proclamations about Skokie, did itself no favors. "We did a very bad job of explaining to the public what we were doing in Skokie," said Burt Neuborne. "I think our public pronouncements were a little too preachy and a little too self-righteous, and we brought down the wrath of a lot of people on us."

The ACLU was attacked from the outside for its history and its stand with the Nazis. Inside there was turmoil as well. The uninhibited Morgan was, as always, gathering headlines with his outspoken way of doing business. When a board member asked the Union's executive director, Aryeh Neier, "How would you control Chuck Morgan?" his reply was, "With difficulty." When a newspaper article appeared parading Morgan's support for a Democratic candidate, Neier worried that this would be taken as ACLU partisanship. Neier, as Morgan tells it, "suggested I be more inhibited in my remarks. I wrote back: no. He wrote asking me what steps I was taking to separate my...views from those of the ACLU. I wrote Neier, 'The step I am taking is to resign.'" The man whom *The New York Times* called "one of the most successful and best known—most loved and hated figures" in the ACLU was gone. Neier himself was tiring of life on the hot seat, and he, too, wished to leave, but ACLU president Dorsen convinced him to stay, at least until Skokie was resolved.

Money was getting tight, and the case in Illinois plodded on into the new year. Finally, on January 27, 1978, the Illinois

State Supreme Court issued its ruling: "We accordingly, albeit reluctantly, conclude that the display of the swastika cannot be enjoined under the fighting-words exception to free speech, nor can anticipation of a hostile audience justify the prior restraint." The Skokie ordinances were ruled unconstitutional, and, in May, the Seventh District Court of Appeals ordered the village to issue the NSPA a permit to assemble. After months of litigation, the ACLU had cleared the way for Frank Collin and his band to demonstrate in front of the village hall in Skokie, in full Nazi regalia. But they didn't show. Justice Department officials, eager to avert problems in Skokie, worked out a compromise in which the NSPA agreed to hold its demonstration at the Federal Plaza in Chicago. They marched there on June 14, 1978, guarded by hundreds of police officers, and met by thousands of counter-demonstrators.

It seems to me," said writer Stanley Fish, "that if you live by the ACLU dictum 'the answer to hate speech is more speech,' what you're going to see is not the end of hate speech, but the proliferation of hate speech, because you will give hate speech more and more of a platform." With respect to Frank Collin, this was true, but only for a short time. He became not so much a celebrity as a curiosity, and was asked to speak at some very respectable forums. Producer Reginald Bryant had him appear on the WHHY-TV show *Black Perspectives on the News*, a public television talk show based in Philadelphia. In his opening statement, Collin told Dr. Lawrence Riddick, an African-American teaching at Harvard, "I definitely regard your race as biologically, genetically, and hopelessly inferior to the white master race."

"I think Skokie was a test for the ACLU," said Norman Siegel. "We lost thousands of members, and we might never get back that particular community and that particular generation. But it was the principled thing to do, and the only thing that the ACLU could have done."

Aryeh Neier, who left the ACLU shortly after Skokie was re-solved, was equally sure the ACLU had done the right thing. "The defense of rights for all, even Nazis, is just what is needed to ensure that Nazism never again prevails," he wrote. But speaking at an ACLU meeting, cartoonist Jules Feiffer asked a tongue-in-cheek question that in a way reflected the Union's exhaustion with the whole thing: "Why can't we come up with a better class of victims? Whatever became of victims like Eugene Debs? Mythic victims. Victims you could hang around with."

Chapter 13

Manger Mania:
The Enduring Battles Over
Separation of Church and State

The ACLU has taken some very tough stands on some very tough issues. I'm one of those examples. And yet there are times when it seems to be more liberal than it does to be libertarian. And there is a difference. And at those moments when principle seems to be thrown to the whim of the political wind it seems to be less effective an organization from my perspective.
—Oliver North

In March 1981, more than fifty years after the Scopes Monkey Trial, the Arkansas senate approved a bill requiring that the Biblical story of Genesis be given equal time with evolution in public school biology classes. Thousands of miles away, a ninety-seven-year-old man was furious. He grabbed his phone. "Did you read about that Arkansas law?" he growled into the receiver. "What are you going to do about it?" With that, the old man smashed the receiver down so hard that the phone fell off the wall. Then he whipped off a press release, denouncing the Arkansas law. Why should anyone care about the ravings of a cantankerous ninety-seven-year-old? Because he was Roger Baldwin.

In theory, Baldwin had been retired for thirty-one years, but for those thirty-one years he had been making almost daily calls to the ACLU office, terrorizing the staff and destroying numerous telephones. Baldwin never quite managed to trust anyone else to direct the struggle for civil liberties in America. And, as he was fond of saying, "No victory ever stays won." Arkansas's new law emphatically proved his case.

To Baldwin, creationism seemed to be nothing more than fundamentalism dressed up in a lab coat. The Arkansas law, the Balanced Treatment for Creation-Science and Evolution-Science Act, was the culmination of ten years of planning and lobbying by a coalition whose main objective was to keep the Christian Bible in the public school curriculum. Creationists had entered the policy arena in the late 1960s, successfully convincing the California Board of Education to issue teacher guidelines for biology courses that gave equal time to Darwin's theory and to the story of creation in Genesis. Both were theories about something that took place in the past, they argued. Both should be given full consideration when biology teachers taught about the beginning of life in biology class. The creation science lobby—which included the Christian Heritage College, the Creation-Life Publishing Company, the Bible Science Association, and an organization called Family, Life, America under God (FLAG)—was gaining influence nationally. In 1980, Ronald Reagan, in his bid for the presidency, said of evolution, "It is not believed in the scientific community to be as infallible as it once was believed. But if it is going to be taught in the schools, then I think the Biblical theory of creation should also be taught." Reagan, of course, was responding to the significant growth of fundamentalist churches in the United States and to the corresponding growth in fundamentalist voters. This group, like the fundamentalists represented by William Jennings Bryan in the 1920s, were feeling nervous about the problems of modern life, particularly modern science. But unlike their Bible-thumping counterparts from the twenties, these groups were politically sophisticated. They knew how to target their efforts. Boards of education and textbook publishers were good places to start. Statehouses were next. Paul Ellwanger, a respiratory therapist who founded the South Carolina-based Citizens for Fairness in Education, considered evolution the cause of many social problems, from Nazism to abortion. "I view this whole battle as one between God and the anti-God forces," he wrote. Convinced that legislation, carefully worded, could both pass in the legislatures and withstand the test of the courts, he crafted a "model" bill and sent it around the country. One such copy reached the hands of James L. Holsted, a self-described "born-again Christian" in the Arkansas State Senate. Without consulting the state department of education or the state's attorney general, he submitted the model bill as Act 590 to the full senate, which passed it without debate. The house sent the bill to the education committee, where it received a cursory going-over. It was passed by the full house and signed by the governor in March 1981.

The ACLU represented a coalition of parents, ministers, and community leaders who challenged the Arkansas law. Their suit claimed that Act 590 violated the First Amendment since its teaching was religious and not scientific. Furthermore, they argued, the law was an illegal curtailment of academic freedom, with dangerously vague language that would give unlimited power to those charged with enforcing it.

Those who came to Little Rock in 1981 looking for an encore of the Scopes trial were a bit disappointed with the proper proceedings. The testimony was, on occasion, interesting—famed scientists Carl Sagan and Stephen Jay Gould took the stand on the ACLU's side and a key witness for the state caused a stir when he announced that UFOs were "satanic manifestations." But, all in all, the trial was a parade of sincere witnesses trying to convince the court that creationism was, or was not, a science. The ACLU called parents, teachers, religious leaders, and specialists in evolution. The state called seven specialists of its own, scientists who, under cross-examination, tended to admit that the science of creationism stemmed solely from the Bible. In January 1982, Judge William R. Overton ruled that the law was "a hodgepodge of limited assertions, many of which are incorrect," and that the idea of balancing evolution and creationism "has no scientific factual basis or legitimate educational purpose." He issued a permanent injunction against the law. But Senator Holsted, even before the ruling was issued, told a reporter from the *Washington Post* that he wasn't worried: "If the law is unconstitutional, it'll just be because some of the language is wrong. . . . We got a lot of time. Eventually, we'll get one that's constitutional." And, indeed, some twenty states were considering similar laws. Still, the judge's ruling was a clear, if temporary, victory. It was also bittersweet. The ACLU's founder was not around for the celebration. Roger Baldwin, grand old man of the American Civil Liberties Union, had died in August 1981 at the age of ninety-seven.

At a memorial service in New York, Norman Dorsen said, "The ancient Greeks maintained that only the good die young. Roger Baldwin's death does not disprove this maxim because he died a young man." It was a contradictory statement, but, then, much of Baldwin's life was made up of contradictions. In his final years he had looked frail, but was sharp, even waspish, in his insistent calls for action on the part of the ACLU. He was suffering from emphysema and heart disease, but joked about "beating the insurance company odds." He spent a good deal of his time during an interview with Mike Wallace of *60 Minutes* talking about how much he enjoyed the company of attractive women. "When I was twenty," he told one interviewer, "I almost died of diphtheria. One night the doctor told me he didn't think I could recover. My attitude then to death was very simple, if you couldn't help it, you face it. I remember I shook hands with the nurse who was watching me through the night, and said good-bye to her. I didn't expect to wake up. Well, I feel the same today."

The year before he died, he received the Medal of Freedom from President Jimmy Carter. He attended the ceremony in a wheelchair, but stood to give a rousing acceptance speech. He said later that there was nothing like a medal to make one feel better quickly. To the end he served as gadfly to the organization he considered his own. At one ACLU event he urged them on, quoting his favorites: Ben Franklin—"Of course the abuses of free speech should be suppressed, but to whom dare we entrust the power to do so"; Learned Hand—"When liberty dies in the hearts of men and women, no constitution, no court, and no law can restore it"; Robert Louis Stevenson—"To travel hopefully is better than to arrive, and the true reward is to labor." He went on from there: "I've been traveling hopefully with you for all these years, and I'm still traveling hopefully. And so is the ACLU. The goal is clear, and the road is hard and progress painful. But we are approaching, we are beginning to approach, a world of peace, order, and justice."

"I remember Baldwin not so much for what he told me to do," said Burt Neuborne, "but for the emotion that would be behind those words: 'Fix it. There's an injustice in the world and it's your job to do something about it.'" Baldwin performed something of a balancing act. He was a moral crusader, but also a canny behind-the-scenes manipulator. He believed that limits to free speech were appropriate in certain political circumstances. He was fully capable of reversing his position on an issue. Some have said that he never made a final commitment to anything: he was a conservative who became a socialist who became a liberal who became a conservative. But he reserved an unbending perseverance, astounding stamina, and stubborn dedication to a cause that, strange to say, needed a champion—the Bill of Rights.

As Arkansas's Senator Holsted had predicted, the creation science coalition continued to work its way through the state legislatures. In Louisiana, a more carefully-worded bill passed, and the ACLU faced a stiffer challenge in defeating that one. They filed suit in 1983, the same year Ronald Reagan proclaimed "The Year of the Bible." Speaking to the National Religious Broadcaster's convention, President Reagan said he had been proud to make such a proclamation. "But a group called the ACLU strongly criticized me for that," he said. "Well, I wear their indictment like a badge of honor." Creationism was an uphill battle for the ACLU, but in 1987 the U.S. Supreme Court ruled that the Louisiana creationism law had been put on the books to "advance the religious viewpoint that a supernatural being created humankind." It was a solid victory for the ACLU, an indication that the Court was, even in the Reagan era, adhering to the clear separation of church and state. Even so, said Anthony Lewis, "creationism is by no means a dead issue." Lewis pinpointed the cause of the religious fervor—the First Amendment itself. "Freedom of religion has made America the most religious of any country in the West," he said. "There is nothing equivalent to the fundamentalist movement in Britain, France, Germany, or Italy. In those countries, state regulation of religion keeps religion more subdued."

Perhaps this explains why every year, in December, the ACLU finds itself in the news. "Some citizen," said Molly Ivins, "suffering from an excess of Christmas spirit, always puts up a religious symbol on public property and the ACLU always sues their ass. Every year I say to them, 'Couldn't you wait until after New Year's?' But no, like the Grinch that stole Christmas, they are suing somebody over an excess of feeling of peace and good will on Earth." This issue of religious decorations on public property has become thornier since some cities have hit on the notion of weaving Christian and Jewish holiday symbols into a large seasonal display, a practice now deemed acceptable by the courts. One ACLU staffer in West Virginia calls the whole thing "manger mania." ACLU members across the state will phone in reports of religious displays on public land, and she will spend a good deal of December driving around, assessing the First Amendment implications of a display that includes a menorah, a crèche, Frosty the Snowman, and Rudolph the Red-Nosed Reindeer. "If Rudolph and Frosty are bigger than the Christ Child, I generally let it go," she said.

It was an irony of the 1980s that the more significant legal battles of the ACLU—abortion rights, anti-censorship, the voting rights project—received a lot less attention than one case, late in the decade, that made for more big headlines than important case law. In 1988, the ACLU filed an *amicus* brief on behalf of Colonel Oliver North in the federal court of appeals in Washington, D.C. North, who had been convicted on perjury charges stemming from his role in the Iran-Contra scandal, proved to be an attention-grabbing case for the ACLU, but also a troublesome one, said Ira Glasser. "All we got was grief for that. Most of our members hated Oliver North's politics."

North had been charged by special prosecutor Lawrence Walsh, who was investigating the rather far-fetched covert operation known as Iran-Contra. It was a National Security Council operation in which profits from the illegal arms sales to Iran were funneled to the Contra rebels fighting the Sandinista government in Nicaragua. Before North's heavily broadcast testimony about the affair before Congress, he had been a shadowy figure, working on such covert operations as the Navy's airborne interception of the *Achille Lauro* hijackers, the U.S. invasion of

Grenada, and the bombing of Libya. North had won two Purple Hearts and the Silver Star during his tour in Vietnam, but even his medals had the air of mystery. The citation for the Silver Star was classified; one source told a *Newsweek* reporter that it involved "something like fighting off a dozen enemy soldiers with a plastic fork." Now at the center of the Iran-Contra scandal, he emerged from the shadows in his heavily decorated uniform to testify—sort of—about his role in the affair. When called before Congress in 1986, North invoked the Fifth Amendment protection against self-incrimination. It was entirely within his rights to do so. It was also infuriating to many in the nation who remembered the injustices done to those who invoked the same privilege during the McCarthy era. "North had a perfect right to take the Fifth," wrote the *New Republic*. "What he has no right to do is to strike a pose of heroic innocence, prattle on about upholding the Constitution, and expect anyone to believe him."

Congress gave North limited immunity in exchange for testimony that would go beyond "I take the Fifth." The independent counsel's office could not use any of his public testimony to build a case against him. In June 1987, North was to be interviewed privately by committee investigators—a step that might have given the committee a chance to craft some narrowly focused questions that would get the information they needed, but still leave room for the special prosecutor to maneuver. But North's attorney managed to avoid the private meetings. The special prosecutor had to build his case with evidence derived in no way from North's testimony. North testified before Congress in 1987. He proved a loquacious, preachy sort of witness, one who bragged about his frequent meetings with the President, misrepresented his academic career, and exaggerated his tour of duty in Vietnam. He said his dog was poisoned by anti-Contra partisans; later it was reported that the dog had died of cancer. The whole affair reminded the nation of Watergate, except, of course, North and his superior, John Poindexter, took the heat off the White House. When it was over, North was out of a job and facing criminal charges, including perjury, from the special prosecutor. "My plans," he said, "are now to trust in the Lord—and a good lawyer."

North had a good lawyer. He also had the support of the ACLU. Their brief in the appeals court argued that the charges against North should be dropped. The colonel's Fifth Amendment rights had been trampled on when he was forced to testify before Congress. Prosecutor Walsh insisted that he and his staff had based their case against North on evidence derived from other sources, and that they had put under seal all evidence accumulated before North testified. They had kept meticulous records throughout, and had even gone so far as to stop reading newspapers or watching TV during the hearings. The ACLU said that that wasn't good enough. The case was just too famous. Neither the prosecution team nor the witnesses could have avoided at least some exposure to North's heavily-reported, much-discussed testimony before Congress. The appeals court agreed and North's case was dismissed. "No other country in the world would give this guy so many chances to get off on technicalities," wrote the *National Review*. "Well," said North, "the technicality they're talking about is the Constitution of the United States. Odious as this may be, it applies equally to you and to me and to John Gotti and to the mobster down the street that's going to get busted for drugs."

North might lump himself together with known criminals, but he had fans all across America. Close to half the people in the country found him "admirable." Perhaps they found his offer to fight terrorist Abu Nidal "anytime, any place, anywhere" endearing. Perhaps they simply believed he was what he said he was, "a patriot." Regardless of the reason, he was a popular man in an election year. He had taken a hit for the president, winning the hearts of many Americans and the praise of several politicians, including Vice President George Bush.

In the summer, immediately after winning the presidential nomination at the Democratic convention, Governor Michael Dukakis looked very strong. He came down the chute full-tilt, chasing the errant Democrats who, in the past two elections, had voted for Ronald Reagan. This was a voting bloc of white men, mostly blue-collar workers uncomfortable with the Jesse Jackson end of the Democratic Party. George Bush needed to keep this vote, and his strategists decided to look for the "hot button issues" that would turn this constituency off Dukakis. Pollster Robert Teeter, in his focus-group work, identified four issues that raised a strong response in these men: the Pledge of Allegiance, gun control, the death penalty, and the ACLU. These were perfect issues: Dukakis was for gun control and opposed to the death penalty; he was also, as the vice president would say many times in the next few months, "a card-carrying member of the ACLU."

It was not clear why the ACLU evinced so visceral a reaction from some voters, but the response at a few speaking engagements told the Bush camp they had something, and they stuck with it all along the campaign trail. In St. Charles, Missouri, Bush intimated that if Dukakis were elected he would consult the ACLU, an "organization out in deep left field," before making appointments to the Supreme Court. The crowd hissed. In Texas, he proclaimed that the ACLU does not reflect "Texas values," and said in Kentucky that the ACLU did not reflect Kentucky values either. "For too many years, we've been held hostage by well-meaning and misguided politicians and judges who get their legal views from the ACLU," said the vice president, and the crowd cheered. In Winston-Salem, North Carolina, Bush suggested that the ACLU hoped to strip the Catholic Church of its tax exemption and repeal kiddie porn laws. In Illinois, Bush said the "left-wingers are getting after me now, but, frankly, I thing it's a good thing we have 'under God' in the Pledge of Allegiance, and I am not going to let them take it away from us." The crowd roared.

That Bush was so successful in his attack on Dukakis's liberal tendencies surprised many, including those in Massachusetts who knew Dukakis well. "Governor Dukakis was not a bleeding heart liberal," said Judith Meredith, author of *The Poor People's Budget* and a well-known welfare advocate in the state. "I am a bleeding heart liberal. Dukakis was an intelligent, competent, boring, middle-of-the-road Democrat." And some people were equally perplexed at the ACLU being a "hot button" issue. "I suppose I'm naive but when George Bush attacked Michael Dukakis as a card-carrying member of the ACLU I was surprised," said Anthony Lewis. "I mean, free speech, what's wrong with that?"

Dukakis dodged the charges of liberalism, and in October, in Jersey City, launched an ACLU attack of his own, listing his disagreements with the Union on issues like pornography, tax exemptions for churches, and Oliver North. Bush promptly accused Dukakis of being a far-out liberal "trying desperately to jump into the mainstream."

Ira Glasser, on a CBS morning news show, said that it was "outrageous" to identify a position for freedom of speech with advocacy of the particular subject the speech concerns. And many of the card-carriers themselves were frustrated at being lumped together in a mass of blind followers of the First Amendment. "The Bush campaign made it seem that membership in the Union meant you supported everything the ACLU ever did," said one member. Such lumping overlooked the internal debates the Union has had since 1920—and also overlooked the fact that the Massachusetts ACLU affiliate had, on a number of occasions, sued Dukakis himself. The Massachusetts Union was then fighting the Governor on a crime sentencing bill that would, according to director John Roberts, "send more people away for longer periods of time." An odd situation, considering that the Bush campaign had successfully painted Dukakis as "soft on crime." In late October, Dukakis was eleven points behind in the polls, and advice poured in from any number of sources. Writing in *Newsweek*, Michael Kramer urged Dukakis to remind voters that Dwight Eisenhower had praised the ACLU. "If I had been Michael Dukakis," said Chuck Morgan, "I would have said that my family comes from Greece, the birthplace of representative democracy. I believe in free speech, and I'm a proud member of the ACLU." Seven years later, advice to Dukakis came in, albeit late, from Hollywood. "Yes!" cried actor Michael Douglas in the movie *The American President*, "I am a card-carrying member of the ACLU. But the more important question is, why aren't you, Bob? This is an organization whose sole purpose is to defend the Bill of Rights." Many felt that Dukakis should have simply acknowledged his membership and be done with it. Republican senator Arlen Specter pegged the issue for the non-issue it was when he said, "There's nothing wrong with belonging to the ACLU."

But in 1988, ACLU membership made more than one politician uncomfortable. When Democratic senator Dennis DeConcini was asked to confirm his membership in the ACLU, his office acknowledged it, then tried to make the senator look less radical by producing a list of conservatives that the Union had defended. Attorney General Richard Thornburgh, Reagan's recent appointee, did some equally quick maneuvering as to his own membership in the ACLU. He essentially apologized for having served on the board of the ACLU in Pennsylvania for two and a half years. Thornburgh had quit the ACLU only when he was appointed U.S. attorney for western Pennsylvania, fearing an appearance of conflict of interest if he stayed on. Bernard Yardoff, who served on the board with him, remembered that Thornburgh gave his "full support" to the ACLU and agreed with its basic principles.

"The presidential race in 1988 was one of the real low points of my life as a citizen of this country," said Molly Ivins. "I can re-member just sitting there sort of frozen, not so much with hor-ror as with sorrow, that being accused of being a supporter of the Bill of Rights could be used against you in a political race." George Bush, who won handily that November, said at one point that he did not want the election to be "a referendum on the ACLU." He admitted that he respected some of its work, but that it "sometimes carries liberal advocacy too far." The irony, of course, was that all the publicity was good for the ACLU. "George Bush was our most successful membership recruiter," said Ira Glasser. "We got nearly sixty thousand new people spon-taneously joining the ACLU, to become card-carrying members, within three months of Bush's attack."

.

Chapter 14

The Right to
Sleep in Bed:
The Chicago Public
Housing Sweeps of 1993

*People in public housing are not saying that they want to
just give up all their right to privacy and let people trample over
their Fourth Amendment rights. We're not saying that at all.
All we are saying is if you're living in dangerous housing, and
if you get killed, what good was the Fourth Amendment? And
the ACLU doesn't seem to care about that.*
                                    —Father George Clements

During the 1980s, it was not uncommon for residents of
Chicago's beleaguered public housing projects to put their
children to bed in the bathtub. Handguns were the weapons of
choice for the drug runners and gang members who had claimed
the projects as their territory, and stray bullets seemed to fly with
frightening regularity in the hallways and courtyards of the high-
rise buildings. The bathtub was, quite simply, the safest place to
sleep. Terror became almost routine to the thousands of
Chicagoans living in housing projects that, since their construction, had been fraught with problems. "The projects were born in

an evil way," said Father George Clements, a Catholic priest and community activist. "They put up those big high-rises to concentrate black people in what was called the 'Black Belt' in Chicago." Harvey Grossman of the Chicago ACLU agreed. "Public housing in the city of Chicago is a separate nation," he said. "The entire construction of public housing in Chicago was geared toward segregating African-Americans, and since 1970, when police officers were shot in public housing, there has never been adequate everyday law enforcement there."

The projects were not only dangerous in 1988, they were broke. Mismanagement had left the Housing Authority in debt to the tune of twelve million dollars. No one was sure how many people really lived in the forty thousand units under Chicago Housing Authority (CHA) control. Turnover was high, partly because an "escalation clause" in the residency agreement automatically raised the rent whenever a tenant's income rose. This meant that working tenants moved out quickly, while the elderly and the very poor stayed behind, essentially forgotten by the city.

By 1988, gangs had taken over three-quarters of the 167 high-rise buildings that made up the city's public housing. It was a rare week that passed without a report of gunfire. "Children were growing up with the sense that they were utterly vulnerable at all times," said Roger Conner. "Their parents couldn't protect them, the superintendent of the Housing Authority couldn't protect them, the police couldn't protect them, the mayor couldn't protect them, God couldn't protect them." Public housing in Chicago was, quite simply, the nation's worst.

Enter Vincent Lane, real estate developer and self-made millionaire, an African-American who had grown up in Chicago, just south of Comisky Park. Lane took charge of the CHA in 1988. Unlike his predecessors, he was a skilled administrator with a gift for getting things done quickly. His first step—firing

the politically connected contractors who provided maintenance and security services to the projects—was welcomed by
the tenants, who had long since given up complaining about elevators that never worked and security guards who were never
around. Lane created his own in-house security police, putting
some of them on the job before their uniforms were ready. Lights
were replaced in the halls and stairwells, elevators were fixed,
garbage was picked up. Tenants were given rent abatements for
patrolling their own buildings.

Slowly, conditions improved, but the violence persisted. In
response, Lane instituted "Operation Clean Sweep." Housing
Authority personnel and Chicago police officers would "sweep"
an entire building, inspecting it, and its residents, from top to
bottom. These were considered "maintenance inspections," but
the CHA officials also checked for "unregistered guests" in the
apartments and enforced a twenty-year-old rule forbidding tenants to keep guns in public housing. If the CHA officials spotted
guns or drugs on the premises, they registered an immediate complaint, and the attending police officers made the arrest on the
spot. By 1992, according to the CHA, crime had fallen by about
30 percent in the swept buildings. Not everyone rejoiced. Subur-
ban politicians worried about the criminals being driven away by
the sweeps. Where would they go? To middle-class neighborhoods in Chicago? To the suburbs? "That would be great," said
Lane. "Nationally, we'll never get a handle on violent crime until
'normal' folks feel the fear that's felt in the ghetto."

Lane and the CHA saw Operation Clean Sweep as both safety
measure and public relations move. They hoped to build a base
of working tenants—stable families that would move to the projects for the affordable rents. Eventually, he hoped, this mixed
population of working families, welfare recipients, and elderly
would displace the gangs that dominated the housing projects.
He knew he would never attract working families to the worst

projects, like Cabrini Green and Robert Taylor Homes, but he also knew that enhanced safety in these crime-ridden buildings would improve the image of public housing throughout the city. He found many who supported his vision. HUD Secretary Jack Kemp funneled more than thirty million dollars into the CHA for programs, including the sweeps. But the Chicago ACLU affiliate protested the warrantless searches. They filed suit to stop the sweeps. Lane simply went to court himself and got a consent decree that allowed the sweeps to continue.

The ACLU was not the only organization to protest. In May 1991, the National Rifle Association (NRA) weighed in with its own complaints about the CHA sweeps. The NRA deputy general counsel, Robert Dowlut, charged that the CHA's gun ban infringed on the residents' Second Amendment right "to keep and bear arms." "Eighty percent of the residents," said Lane, "are single mothers, with children, on welfare. I can tell you they are not out hunting pheasant or taking target practice. The only use of weapons in the housing projects is for negative reasons."

It was an unusual occurrence—the ACLU and the NRA coming down on the same side of an issue. In the past, the NRA had roundly criticized the ACLU for its unwillingness to promote gun ownership as a civil liberty in America. Gun ownership, the NRA argued, is protected under the Second Amendment to the Constitution, and should therefore be on the ACLU's shortlist of issues. Many gun advocates were perturbed by the ACLU's position. "The ACLU ought to be taking on my Second Amendment right to bear arms," said Oliver North. The ACLU president, Nadine Strossen, disagreed. "We are neutral on the issue of gun control," she said. "The only way we support the NRA is in its First Amendment right to speak about its position on owning guns and other weapons."

In explaining its position on gun ownership, the ACLU said

that it was in agreement with the Supreme Court decision *U.S. v. Miller*. This decision, handed down in 1939, stated that the Second Amendment's brief text—"A well-regulated Militia, being necessary to the security of a free State, the right of the people to keep and bear Arms, shall not be infringed"—was meant to guarantee the state's right to maintain a militia, not the individual's right to keep a gun.

The ACLU and the NRA are clearly at odds on the Second Amendment, but they resemble one another in their willingness to take the extreme, abstract position in defense of their respective causes. The NRA is ready to oppose any gun control ordinance, even the weakest, in their firm belief that any restriction will eventually give way to larger measures. The ACLU reacts the same way to restrictions on civil liberties—any incursion, even a small one, could result in greater incursions in the future and must be fought. "The ACLU," said Roger Conner, "defends positions which seem very extreme on the grounds that if we take one step in this direction we'll fall down the 'slippery slope' into a fascist state. This 'slippery slope' thinking has gotten such control over their minds that they've lost their common sense."

Both the ACLU and the NRA have appeared almost rabid in their defense of their respective causes, particularly when, as in the Chicago sweeps case, they are intervening in a neighborhood where few, if any, of their constituents lived. The NRA, said the chief of the CHA police, "never cared about black people before." Father Clements leveled a similar charge at the ACLU. "How can an overwhelmingly white organization claim to represent a whole group of black people? They have no ties to public housing whatsoever, other than their academic approach to it. Yet they can claim that they're representing the people."

The ACLU had challenged sweep searches before. In 1984, the Detroit school board, in response to the growing violence in their high schools, conducted a number of surprise sweeps in schools throughout the city. In the sweeps, school security guards and Detroit police searched students for weapons, using hand-held and walk-through metal detectors. It was an extreme measure, but the precipitating violence had been equally extreme. There had been seventy felonious assaults on students and teachers in one year alone.

The Michigan chapter of the ACLU went to court to stop the sweeps, charging that the weapons searches were unconstitutional: the searches were randomly staged, warrantless, and conducted on individuals under no particular suspicion. The federal district judge who heard the case ordered a temporary halt to the sweeps. The school board set up a new program that targeted the most violent schools and eliminated the police. School security guards were to carry out the searches alone. In a move that seemed to guarantee that the searches would yield nothing, the school board announced in advance when the sweeps would take place. But the ACLU said it would oppose any random searches, and the school board backed away from the sweeps altogether.

Then, in 1987, a fourteen-year-old student shot an eighteen-year-old star athlete at point-blank range after an argument at school. Some in the city placed the blame for the student's death squarely on the ACLU. Others blamed the school board for caving in to the ACLU's demands. The school board brought the metal detectors back and started sweeping again, albeit in a more limited way. The ACLU chose not to contest the searches, but argued that the authorities would get more weapons out of the schools if they would use the money spent on the sweeps in search programs that investigated only students under actual suspicion of gun possession. Sweeps, said the ACLU, were essentially ineffective.

But sweeping was an appealing idea, particularly to politicians trying to halt the violence that seemed to come directly from guns and illegal drugs in America. During his chairmanship of the Texas War on Drugs Committee, Ross Perot called for a "civil war" and suggested that police go into high crime neighborhoods, cordon off the area, then search block by block, house by house, for guns and drugs. Perot's idea was clearly a violation of any number of civil liberties. During the 1992 election, when even Vice President Dan Quayle, not known for his libertarian concerns, accused the Texas millionaire of gutting the Constitution, Perot disavowed the sweeps idea. But he, along with the whole field of presidential candidates, came out for stiffer measures that would stop crime and improve public safety, because these issues had emerged as the "hot button" issues in the 1992 presidential race.

Here again, the ACLU was assuming an unpopular stance. It opposed stricter policing laws and questioned public safety measures that enjoyed widespread support. At one time or another, the ACLU has fought metal detectors in airports, sobriety checkpoints on the highways, and random drug testing in the workplace, even for railway engineers and truck drivers. "When you ask them why," said Roger Conner, "it's because it's taking away individual rights. Their notion of rights is individual, absolute, and disconnected from any sense of social obligation."

The summer of 1993 must have seemed like war in some of the housing projects of Chicago. The gangs had regrouped, and the shooting was, once again, routine. In the Robert Taylor Homes project, there were three hundred reports of shootings that year; in another housing project, police said some innocent bystander had been shot at once a day, had been hit once a week, and had been killed once a month. Artensa Randolph, the president of the CHA Tenant's Association, lived in an apartment flanked on either side by drug dealers. "Naturally I'm afraid," she said. "When they hear those shots, everybody, the parents and the children, are afraid. They fall on the floor, they get in the bathtub, anywhere they can hide."

That summer, the Chicago Police Department and the Chicago Housing Authority conducted a program of aggressive sweeps. These were intentionally dramatic events, staged to send a message to the gangs and drug dealers and to calm the ever-growing fears of the residents. Armed police surrounded the buildings and stopped anyone trying to enter or leave. They posted officers on every stairwell and porch, then marched inside to search every apartment on every floor. They went through over twelve hundred apartments this way, and as Harvey Grossman of the ACLU tells it, they turned the apartments upside down. "They went through people's drawers, through their closets, through their bedclothes in blatantly illegal fashion," he said. "The Fourth Amendment prohibits these kinds of searches. That's the same guarantee that people in private housing have— in the absence of a warrant or probable cause, the Fourth Amendment prohibits the search of a home."

As in Detroit, the ACLU said the sweeps were not only unconstitutional, they were ineffective. The typical search, according to one reporter, yielded only a "a windfall of handguns chucked out the upper story window." The ACLU said that weapons were brought back into the same buildings within days. One tenant claimed the guns were back within minutes. Regardless of effect, the sweeps brought a measure of comfort to many of the public housing tenants. "Our residents welcomed the sweeps," said Artensa Randolph. "They told me they could sleep at night."

But not all tenants felt safer. "For me, personally, the searches were pretty demeaning," said Mark Pratt. "I was searched twice, thoroughly. In my underwear, my shoes. They attempted to search my two-year-old son." Ethyl Washington of the Robert Taylor Homes project was downright furious. "How would you like for somebody to just walk into your house and search your belongings?" she asked. "They were flipping around my papers, and looking in my encyclopedia. I told them to get out of my apartment."

The ACLU was on familiar territory—representing an unpopular minority. Pratt and Washington both sought help from the ACLU, and signed on with the class action suit that the Union brought against Chicago, but they were among a mere handful of residents who did so. "The ACLU found a few people, four to be exact, who represented their views," said Father Clements. "And they claim from those four that they were representing the entire class of all the public tenants of public housing. Such arrogance, to go into court and claim that you have a class action suit." For his part, Mark Pratt felt that the low number of tenants siding with the ACLU reflected the fact that many of the tenants did not understand the implications of the sweeps. "I held two impromptu meetings with residents in my building," he said, "and informed them of the terms of the consent decree and what their rights were. They were shocked that the things that took place within their apartments were unconstitutional." But Artensa Randolph argued that the ACLU was putting the abstract rights of a few people ahead of the concrete reality of families decimated by gunfire and fear. "Do they want us to live with gunshots?" she asked. "I frankly don't understand those people."

Grossman acknowledged that the ACLU took the minority position. "It's very easy to accept the proposition of majority will," he said. "One is forced to take strong stands when you seek to represent minorities or unpopular positions. That

doesn't make us wrong. It simply makes us unpopular." Vince
Lane, however, was finding considerable support, in Chicago
and across the country. Other major cities watched closely.
From Washington, President Bill Clinton spoke favorably about
the program. "We shouldn't let...the criminal population ter-
rorize the country," he said. "The President," responded Ethyl
Washington, "is not going to let anybody come in into the
White House to search his house and his family."

The courts, after two years of litigation, sided with Ethyl
Washington. The ACLU had won, and Grossman insisted they
had won in a responsible manner. "We did not run willy-nilly
into the CHA and challenge a search because, as a technical
matter, it violated the Fourth Amendment," he said. "We hired
law enforcement consultants, seasoned veterans of the streets of
New York, and the public housing authorities of New York.
They told us that this was not a solution. They told us that
there were proper methods to be employed that would be effective. And it is those methods that we recommended in the
courtroom." The Housing Authority can no longer enter an individual's apartment without a warrant or consent. They must
limit their searches to the common areas of the building—the
stairwells, elevators, and hallways. "They can't barge their way
into your home, like the Gestapo did in Germany in the
1930s," said Mark Pratt.

The Housing Authority has plans to demolish the worst of the
highrises, and to relocate the residents to other parts of Chicago.
This might defuse the violence, but for some residents this measure is simply too late. "I'm going to mention a name that I'm absolutely certain that nobody at the ACLU has ever even heard
of," Father Clements said during his interview. "The name is
'Andre Brit.' Andre Brit had a family at 48–44 South State
Street in Chicago. Andre was on the walkway, the balcony outside his apartment, one evening when all of a sudden, gunfire

started. A bullet hit him right in the chest. He was killed instantly. His wife and his children were standing near him when it happened. Andre is dead. We had his funeral at our church. He's gone." Father Clements shakes his head sadly. "Fourth Amendment. Try to talk about the Fourth Amendment to Mrs. Brit and to her children."

Chapter 15

The Orderly Progress
of Civil Liberties

*We shouldn't win all of our arguments. We should win a
large number of them, but we shouldn't win them all. There
has to be some sort of balance between the needs of the individual and the needs of the group. What Roger Baldwin did
was invent this marvelous machine for making that balance:
the ACLU on one side, arguing as hard as it can in favor of
individualism, the government on the other, articulating the
needs for collective power, and the courts making the final
decision. That's the way we worked this out in this century,
and it's worked out quite well.*

—Burt Neuborne

Roger Baldwin founded the American Civil Liberties Union
in 1920 with a handful of political friends and a few hundred dollars. In that first year, the Union pledged itself to "an aggressive policy of insistence" in the name of civil liberties. "We
stand," Baldwin wrote in the Union's original statement of purpose, "on the principle that all thought on matters of public
concern should be freely expressed, without interference. Orderly social progress is promoted by unrestricted freedom of
speech. The punishment of mere opinion, without overt acts, is
never in the interest of orderly progress." No doubt, Baldwin

chose to embed "orderly progress" in this plan of action because the times were so disorderly. The ACLU was founded just two weeks after the draconian Palmer raids took place, thousands of Americans were in jail for "speech crimes," and, throughout the country, police were riding roughshod over the First Amendment's guarantees of freedom of speech, press, and assembly. The executive and legislative branches of the federal government colluded on unfair arrests and searches and seizures. The U.S. Supreme Court had never struck down a speech case on First Amendment grounds in its 150-year history.

Baldwin believed America's disorder stemmed from the government's unwillingness to support the individual freedoms guaranteed in the Bill of Rights. "The country is going wild," he said. "We need an organization to fight for civil liberties." Liberty was the goal of the ACLU—order would be the outcome.

Almost eight decades later, any number of critics now charge that the ACLU has turned its back on all notions of "orderly progress" and has adopted instead a radical adherence to individual rights at any cost. "An old nursery rhyme we all learned is relevant to the ACLU's current position," said Stanley Fish. "'Sticks and stones will break my bones, but words will never hurt me' is the position the ACLU takes with regard to free speech. But it has to be rewritten to conform to modern events. 'Sticks and stones may break my bones, but detailed instructions on the Internet on how to build plutonium bombs so that fourteen-year-olds can download the plans and build a bomb won't hurt me.' When the old proverb is redone that way, I think you can see why free speech does not mean today what it meant in 1920."

The supporters and critics of the ACLU now air their differences in an arena that has placed order and safety in one corner, individual liberties in the other. "It's not right versus wrong," said Roger Conner. "It's the collision of a set of values which are good. Strong communities are good. Individual autonomy is good. When these competing good values collide with each other, it's going to produce friction and battle." Since the late 1960s, the ACLU has been consistently colliding with so many organizations that its very name has become synonymous with trouble. Little wonder. They have sued hundreds of local governments and school boards over issues ranging from voting rights to Christmas pageants. They have sued companies wanting to run drug tests on their employees and hospitals unwilling to treat people with AIDS. They sued the Citadel on behalf of women who wanted in, and have sued states on behalf of convicted prisoners who want to get out. They claim to defend everybody; at times, it seems, they are suing everybody, even their friends. The ACLU has gotten along pretty well with the Clinton administration. Still, they are fighting the administration on several fronts, including public housing sweeps, the anti-terrorism bill, and the death penalty. "We protect victims first and make criminals pay for their crimes," said presidential advisor Rahm Emmanuel in 1996. "That may get us in the crosshairs of the ACLU, but those are our principles."

That the Clinton administration would distance itself from the ACLU in an election year is not surprising. It is unlikely that any candidate, even an incumbent president, would brag about a good relationship with the ACLU; it continues to be a "hot button" issue with voters. "The ACLU?" said an Arizona woman at the polls in 1996. "Those are the 'save the plankton' whackos, right?" In his HBO special of the same year, comedian Dennis Miller accused the Union of spearheading the 'soft on crime' movement that's ruining America. "I hear the ACLU wants us to call the killer bees the 'manslaughter bees,'" he said. "Well, if you ask me, the ACLU doesn't have a fucking A-C-L-U-E, okay?" And in *The New York Times*, writer James Atlas said that he tosses any ACLU literature the minute it comes through the mail slot. "The first thing I throw away are all those worthy solicitations," he wrote, "especially the ACLU. I don't consider porn shops in my neighborhood a First Amendment right."

Admirers say the ACLU is the best watchdog we have for protecting the rights granted by the Constitution; detractors insist it uses a warped version of what the Constitution says. "The central purpose of the government created under the Constitution," said Nadine Strossen, ACLU president, "was to aid individuals in preserving their freedom, 'to secure the blessings of liberty.'" Roger Conner disagrees. "Go back and read the Preamble to the Constitution," he said. "'To form a more perfect union.' It's for the creation of a community where there is an exchange of rights and obligations."

Admired or despised, the ACLU is probably the most powerful legal organization in America. With 250,000 members, it now takes on some six thousand cases a year. "One of the great misconceptions that the ACLU has about itself," said Roger Conner, "is that they're David versus Goliath. Quite the opposite is true. The ACLU comes into these battles with lawyers, briefs, an elaborate network, and an enormous amount of money. Their opponent is usually a small-town lawyer who works part-time for the city. The ACLU is Goliath."

The ACLU's 1920 Statement of Purpose spelled out its position "on issues in the United States today": "freedom of speech, press, and assemblage ... must be reasserted in its application to American conditions today." Those were the bedrock liberties that Baldwin was determined to defend. "I suppose," he said in 1980, "you can now stretch civil liberties to cover a large number of things that the Bill of Rights never contemplated." In his own lifetime Baldwin had seen the meaning of civil liberties stretched considerably beyond a point he himself had ever contemplated. In that way, he was in the same boat with the man who drafted the Bill of Rights, James Madison. Neither had ever given any thought to censorship on the Internet, or metal detectors in airports, but what does that matter? "The Bill of Rights is a living document," said Molly Ivins. "It's not just a bunch of old words written down somewhere that sits there in perpetuity. Every generation, you have to fight to make it work. You have to fight to make it real."

Where exactly does the ACLU stand on the issues that have emerged in modern life? At times it's difficult to tell. The ACLU comes out four square in favor of women's reproductive rights, including the right to abortion. But Ira Glasser cautions against seeing the issue as one of abortion rights only. "In the future," he said, "reproductive freedom may be the right to bear children if the government decides to limit childbirth as a means of controlling population." But the ACLU also supports the rights of the pro-life movement to picket at abortion clinics, including the right of protesters to use speech to persuade women not to go ahead with the procedure. "That's protected speech," said Glasser. "It's a First Amendment right." However, said Chester Darling, an attorney from Boston, "The ACLU is not terribly industrious in defending the rights of the people protesting in front of abortion clinics."

Roger Baldwin looked downright squeamish talking about another modern civil liberties issue. "It's only in recent years the ACLU has looked at homosexual rights, when they, as they say, came out of the closet. Before that, we shied off from it. We thought it was a rather distasteful aspect of civil liberties, and our board did not want to take up that kind of case." Since then, the ACLU seems to be making up for lost time, sponsoring an ongoing gay and lesbian rights project and taking on a hefty load of gay and lesbian cases. The ACLU has lobbied to change President Clinton's "don't ask, don't tell" military policy, saying that "it effectively continues the military's ban on gay and les-

bian service," and have fought ballot initiatives aimed at limiting gay and lesbian rights in the community. In the early 1990s,
the ACLU supported the rights of gays to march openly in
Boston's publicly sponsored St. Patrick's Day Parade, but at the
same time supported a Hibernian group in New York that
wished to hold a private parade that excluded gays. "No one expected the Civil Liberties Union to be on the side of the Hibernians," said Norman Siegel of the New York Civil Liberties
Union. "But the City of New York was not going to issue a permit to the Hibernians unless they allowed gay groups to march
in what was essentially a private parade. African-Americans, for
example, have every right to stage a privately-funded parade
that excludes members of the KKK. It's a free speech issue. We
cannot allow the government to tell people whom they have to
march with and what message they must express."

For years the ACLU has campaigned for liberal advertising
laws for tobacco companies, even as public health officials were
condemning cigarettes as a deadly American passion. The
ACLU has been criticized severely for defending the tobacco
industry's rights, not only because smoking is unhealthy, but
also because the Union has been on the receiving end of a considerable sum of the tobacco money. Between 1986 and 1996 it
received some $920,000 in donations from tobacco companies.
Glasser points out that the donations come in with no strings
attached, and that the ACLU is free to accept money from
whomever it chooses. "We'd accept money from John Gotti,"
he said. But critics counter that, in this case, the ACLU is
fighting to protect commercial speech, not political speech.
Commercial speech has always been subject to government regulation and the ACLU's spirited defense of advertising rights is,
for some, an indication of the organization's willingness to sell
out. Glasser insists that the ACLU must fight the government
whenever it attempts to regulate speech. "What's the alterna-

tive?" he asks. "It's to give the government the power to decide which speech to allow and which speech to prohibit. Every citizen must ultimately ask him or herself this question: 'What's your worst political nightmare?' Maybe it's Pat Buchanan, maybe it's Bill Clinton. Do you want that person deciding which speech to allow and which speech to prohibit?" But don't we elect our government? "In a sense," said Stanley Fish, "the ACLU is profoundly anti-democratic. It does not trust Americans to elect people who will do the right kind of regulating. It distrusts the democratic process."

In the long run, the ACLU has the advantage in any debate because it can comfortably take the absolutist position: civil liberties must be defended at all costs. Nobody is willing to argue the opposite position—that we should abandon freedom in this country altogether. And every critic must concede that the ACLU has done good work. Even George Bush acknowledged that some of their efforts were admirable, and there is a general agreement that our late twentieth-century definition of liberty has come, in large part, from the ACLU. Justice Oliver Wendell Holmes once wrote that the Constitution "is an experiment, as all life is an experiment." For better or worse, the ACLU, and America, are still tinkering with the meaning of freedom.

"The United States, in civil liberties terms," said Anthony Lewis, "is a freer country than any on earth. Does this mean the ACLU can go to bed, can go away to live happily ever after? Of course not. The reason we are free is because the ACLU and a few other organizations are constantly on the lookout." Roger Baldwin, of course, would agree. "The struggle for civil liberties is never won," he said. "It's a struggle that's day by day, every day. And it begins every morning."

Bibliography

NOTE: The most recently published history of the ACLU is also the most extensive: *In Defense of American Liberties*, written by Samuel Walker, was published in 1990 and will be reissued this year; intensely researched and detailed, Professor Walker recounts hundreds of ACLU battles and his book is an invaluable resource. An earlier work, *The Pulse of Freedom*, edited by Alan Reitman in 1975, lays out in essay form the history and issues that the ACLU contended with since its inception. There are dozens of other works as well; the ones I consulted are listed in the bibliography below. Some of the constitutional discussions on free speech and other civil liberties can be hard going for laypersons like myself. Those interested in a readable introduction to the Bill of Rights are encouraged to read Anthony Lewis's *Make No Law: The Sullivan Case and the First Amendment*; Ellen Alterman and Caroline Kennedy's study on the Bill of Rights, *In Our Defense*; and Ira Glasser's *Visions of Liberty*.

The Mudd Library at Princeton University has an extensive and accessible collection of ACLU manuscripts, photographs, and publications. Other sources are listed in the film archival credits below.

Selected Books

Beaver, Daniel R. *Newton D. Baker and the American War Effort, 1917–1919*. Lincoln: University of Nebraska Press, 1966.

Biddle, Francis. *In Brief Authority*. New York: Doubleday, 1962.

Boyer, Paul S. *Purity in Print: The Vice-Society and Book Censorship in America*. New York: Charles Scribner's Sons, 1968.

Collins, Donald E. *Native American Aliens: Disloyalty and the Renunciation of Citizenship by Japanese Americans during World War II*. Westport: Greenwood Press, 1985.

Cook, Blanche Wiesen, ed. *Crystal Eastman on Women and Revolution*. Oxford: Oxford University Press, 1978.

Creel, George. *How We Advertised America*. New York: Harper and Brothers, 1920.

Darwin, Charles. *Journal of Researches into the Natural History and Geology of the Countries Visited During the Voyage of HMS Beagle Round the World*. New York: Appleton and Co., 1876.

Donohue, William. *Twilight of Liberty: The Legacy of the ACLU*. New Jersey: Transaction Press, 1994.

Downs, Donald Alexander. *Nazis in Skokie: Freedom, Community and the First Amendment*. Indiana: University of Notre Dame Press, 1985.

Ernst, Morris. *The Censor Marches On*. New York: Doubleday, Doran & Co., 1940.

Fish, Stanley. *There's No Such Thing as Free Speech...and it's a good thing too*. New York:, Oxford University Press, 1994.

Glasser, Ira. *Visions of Liberty: The Bill of Rights for All Americans*. New York: Arcade Publishing, 1991.

Ginger, Ray. *Six Days or Forever?: Tennessee v. John Thomas Scopes*. New York: Oxford University Press, 1958.

Hamlin, David. *The Nazi Skokie Conflict: A Civil Liberties Battle*. Boston: Beacon Press, 1980.

Hays, Arthur Garfield. *City Lawyer: The Autobiography of a Law Practice*. New York: Simon and Schuster, 1942.

Irons, Peter. *The Courage of Their Convictions: Sixteen Americans Who Fought Their Way to the Supreme Court.* New York: The Free Press, 1988.

Jackson, Kenneth T. *The Ku Klux Klan in the City, 1915–1930.* New York: Oxford University Press, 1967.

Johnson, Donald. *The Challenge to American Freedom: World War I and the Rise of the ACLU.* Lexington: University of Kentucky, 1963.

Lamson, Peggy. *Roger Baldwin: Founder of the American Civil Liberties Union.* Boston: Houghton Mifflin Company, 1976.

Lewis, Anthony. *Make No Law: The Sullivan Case and the First Amendment.* New York: Random House, 1992.

Mahin, Helen Ogden, ed. *The Editor and His People: Editorials Selected by William Allen White.* New York: MacMillan Company, 1924.

Marchand, C. Roland. *The American Peace Movement and Social Reform, 1898–1918.* New Jersey: Princeton University Press, 1972.

McAuliffe, Mary Sperling. *Crisis on the Left: Cold War Politics and American Liberals, 1947–1954.* Amherst: University of Massachusetts Press, 1978.

McKean, David. *The Boss: The Hague Machine in Action.* Boston: Houghton Mifflin Company, 1940.

Milner, Lucille. *Education of an American Liberal.* New York: Horizon Press, 1954.

Morgan, Charles. *A Time to Speak.* New York: Holt, Rinehart and Winston, 1964.

———. *One Man, One Voice.* New York:, Holt, Rinehart and Winston, 1979.

Mock, James R., and Cedric Larson. *Words That Won the War: The Story of the Committee on Public Information, 1917–1919.* Princeton: Princeton University Press, 1939.

Murray, Robert K. *Red Scare: A Study in National Hysteria, 1919–1920*. St. Paul: University of Minnesota Press, 1955.

Neier, Aryeh. *Defending my Enemy: American Nazis, the Skokie Case, and the Risks of Freedom*. New York: E. P. Dutton, 1979.

Palmer, Frederick. *Newton D. Baker, America at War*. New York: Dodd, Mead & Co., 1931.

Patriotism Through Education Series, No. 9, New York: National Security League, 1918.

Powers, Richard God. *Secrecy and Power: The Life of J. Edgar Hoover*. New York: The Free Press, 1987.

Reitman, Alan, ed. *The Pulse of Freedom*. New York: W.W. Norton, 1975.

Scopes, John Thomas, and James Presley. *Center of the Storm: Memoirs of John T. Scopes*. New York: Holt, Rinehart and Winston, 1967.

Singerman, Robert. *Antisemitic Propaganda: An Annotated Bibliography and Research Guide*. New York: Garland Publishing, Inc., 1982.

Thomas, Norman. *The Conscientious Objector*. New York: B.W. Huebsch, 1923.

Tompkins, Jerry R., ed. *D-Days at Dayton: Reflections on the Scopes Trial*. Baton Rouge: Louisiana State University Press, 1965.

Walker, Samuel. *In Defense of American Liberties: A History of the ACLU*. New York: Oxford University Press, 1990.

Yespen, Roger. *Apples*. New York: Norton, 1994.

Selected Articles and Periodicals

"The ACLU & the FBI: Over 50 Years of Constant Surveillance." *The Civil Liberties Review* (November/December 1977).

Alter, Jonathan. "When Sources Get Immunity—Was North Pampered?" *Newsweek* (January 19, 1987).

American Civil Liberties Union. Reprint, U.S. Congress—House Committee on Rules. "Do We Need More Sedition Laws?" Testimony of Alfred M. Bettman and Swinbure Hale (1921).

"Another Repeal." *The Nation* (December 20, 1933).

"The Anti-Evolution Trial in Tennessee." *School and Society* (July 11, 1925).

"Are American Liberties Worth Saving? Letters from New York Lawyers." *The Nation* 110, no. 2859.

"Armed Forces: Men at War." *Time* (June 2, 1967).

Baer, Donald, and Melissa Healy. "What Will Ollie Say—and When?" *U.S. News and World Report* (June 29, 1987).

"The Baiting of Judge Raulston." *The New Republic* (July 29, 1925).

Baldwin, Roger Nash. "Free Speech for Nazis?" *World Tomorrow* 16 (November 9, 1933).

———. "Recollection of a Life in Civil Liberties—I." *The Civil Liberties Review* 2, no. 2 (1975).

———. "Recollections of a Life in Civil Liberties—II: Russia, Communism, and United Fronts, 1920–1940." *The Civil Liberties Review* 2, no. 4 (1975).

"Barenblatt Case and Congressional Investigations," *Science* (May 9, 1958).

Bennet, James. "ACLU Too, Buddy." *The New Republic* (October 17, 1988).

Brooks, Van Wyck. "Harvard And American Life." *The Contemporary Review* (November 8, 1908).

"Candidate Debs is a Beneficent Influence in Prison, But Still A Revolutionist." *The Literary Digest* (October 23, 1920).

"Censorship As Finally Enacted." *The Survey* (June 9, 1917).

Chafee, Zechariah, Jr. "Freedom of Speech." *The New Republic* (November 16, 1918).

"Civil Rights: Opening a Second Front." *Newsweek* (November 8, 1965).

Cohen, Carl. "Skokie—The Extreme Test." *The Nation* (April 15, 1978).

"The Communist Arrests." *New Republic* (August 2, 1948).

"Conscientious Objectors and How To Treat Them." *Living Age* (July 1, 1916).

"Conscription and Eugenics." *The Independent* (February 7, 1916).

"The Conviction of John Thomas Scopes, Science Teacher." *School and Society* (August 1, 1925).

"The Court-Martial of Captain Levy: Medical Ethics v. Military Law." *Science* 156 (June 9, 1967).

"Courts-Martial: Nuremberg Revisited." *Newsweek* (May 29, 1967).

De Silver, Albert. "The Great Battle for Amnesty." *The Nation* (January 2, 1924).

Dewey, John. "Freedom of Thought and Work." *The New Republic* (May 5, 1920).

"The Doctors' Dilemma." *The Nation* (May 29, 1967).

"The Duke of Flux." *The Nation* (October 17, 1988).

Durant, Will. "Why Freedom Disappears." *The Nation* (May 1, 1920).

"Facts About Faces: I. Roger Baldwin." *The New Republic* (January 2, 1935).

"Fifth Amendment Patriots." *The New Republic* (January 5 and 12, 1987).

"Friends Meet In Memory of Roger Baldwin." *Vineyard Gazette* (October 1981).

"Georgia: Right to Speak." *Time* (December 16, 1966).

"Georgia: The Bond Issue." *Time* (February 18, 1966).

Glastris, Paul. "The ACLU and the Right to Die in a Train Wreck...One That Should Be The Best, But Isn't." *The Washington Monthly* (March 1988).

———. "Chicago's Housing Czar." *U.S. News and World Report* (August 26/September 2, 1991).

Goldberger, David. "Clients Everyone Hates." *Litigation* (Spring 1995).

"Guilty as Charged." *Time* (June 9, 1967).

Hamlin, David M. "Swastikas & Survivors: Inside the Skokie-Nazi Free Speech Case." *The Civil Liberties Review* (March/April 1978).

Hays, Arthur Garfield. "The Strategy of the Scopes Defense." *The Nation* 121, no. 3135.

Healy, Melissa, with Ted Gest. "What Will They Say—and When?" *U.S. News and World Report* (March 23, 1987).

Hoke, Travis. "Red Rainbow." *The North American Review* (November 1932).

Holmes, John Haynes. "Belated Aid for Objectors." *The New Republic* (March 15, 1919).

Huxley, Julian. "Will Science Destroy Religion?" *Harpers Magazine* (April 1926).

Kauffmann, Stanley. "Operation Abolition." *New Republic* (March 27, 1961).

Kirchwey, Freda. "Curb the Fascist Press!" *The Nation* (March 28, 1942).

Kramer, Michael. "A Memo to Michael Dukakis." *U.S. News and World Report* (October 17, 1988).

Kramer, Michael. "See No Evil, Hear No Evil, Speak No Evil." *U.S News and World Report* (July 27, 1987).

———. "Perot's Smart Idea." *Time* (July 6, 1992).

Krutch, Joseph Wood. "Darrow vs. Bryan." *The Nation* (July 29, 1925).

Lane, Winthrop D. "Who Are the Conscientious Objectors?" *The New Republic* (April 14, 1920).

Livingstone, Neil C. "What Ollie North Told Me Before He Took the Fifth." *National Review* (January 30, 1987).

"Malin to Direct Civil Liberties Union." *The Christian Century* (January 11, 1950).

Marro, Anthony. "F.B.I. Files Disclose '50s Tie to ACLU." *The New York Times* (August 4, 1977).

Martz, Larry, with Margaret Garbard Warner, Howard Fineman, Eleanor Clift, and Mark Starr. "The Smear Campaign." *Newsweek* (October 31, 1988).

McCormick, John. "Chicago Housecleaning." *Newsweek* (August 19, 1991).

McGeehan, W.O. "Why Pick on Dayton?" *Harper's Monthly Magazine* (October 1925).

"The Menace of Sedition." *Public Opinion* (September 1, 1917).

Mencken, H.L. "In Tennessee." *The Nation* (July 1, 1925).

Moon, Robert. "Operation Abolition." *The Christian Century* (January 4, 1961).

Morganthau, Tom, with Kim Willenson and Rod Nordland in Washington and Thomas M. De Frank with Reagan in Santa Barbara. "Trusting 'in the Lord and a Good Lawyer.'" *Newsweek* (December 8, 1986).

Muirhead, James F. "The Zeppelin Raid-Conscription: A Summary of the Arguments for and Against Compulsory Service." *The Nation* (September 30, 1915).

Mumford, Lewis. "Patriotism and Its Consequences." *The Dial* (April 19, 1919).

Neier, Aryeh. "Engagement and the German-Jewish Legacy." *American Jewish Archives* (1988).

Nelkin, Dorothy. "Creationism Evolves." In *The Creation Controversy: Science or Scriptures in the Schools*. New York: Norton, 1982.

O'Connor, John. "Communism-America's Menace." *Vital Speeches of the Day* (broadcast June 10, 1938).

"Ollie's Allies." *The New Republic* (August 29, 1988).

Pearson, Richard. "Roger Baldwin, A Founder of ACLU, Dies." *The Washington Post* (August 27, 1981).

"Policies & Principles, Trial Balance." *Time* (July 14, 1947).

Preston, Charles, Jr. "The 1940s: The Way We Really Were." *The Civil Liberties Review* (Winter 1975).

Preston, William, Jr. "By Life Possessed: The Dissenter as Hero." *Reviews in American History* (September 1977).

"The Progress of Civil Liberty in the United States." *The Nation* (April 6, 1921).

Prud'Homme, Alex. "Chicago's Uphill Battle." *Time* (June 17, 1991).

"Quotations: The Anti-Evolution Trial in Tennessee." *Science* (July 17, 1925).

"Right to Inquire." *U.S. News and World Report* (January 11, 1958).

"Roger Baldwin Dies; Founder of ACLU." *St. Louis Post-Dispatch* (August 26, 1981).

"Roger Baldwin, 97, Is Dead; Crusader for Civil Rights Founded the ACLU." *The New York Times* (August 27, 1981).

Rolo, Charles. "Cultural Resistance." *The Saturday Review* (January 8, 1949).

Rostow, Eugene V. "Our Worst Wartime Mistake." *Harper's Magazine* (September 1945).

Salisbury, Harrison, E. "The Strange Correspondence of Morris Ernst and John Edgar Hoover 1939–1964." *The Nation* (December 1, 1984).

Samuels, Gertrude. "The Fight for Civil Liberties Never Stays Won." *The New York Times Magazine* (June 19, 1966).

"Science in the News." *Science* (November 20, 1959).

"Science in the News: Committee Assesses Dangers That Accompany Government Support of University Research." *Science* 131 (March 11, 1960).

Shapiro, Herbert. "Julian Bond: Georgia's 'Uppity' Legislator." *The Nation* (February 7, 1966).

Simmons, Jerold. "The Origins of the Campaign to Abolish HUAC, 1956–1961, The California Connection." *Historical Society of Southern California* (1982).

———. "Morris Ernst and Disclosure: One Liberal's Quest for a Solution to the Problem of Domestic Communism, 1939–1949." *Mid-America, An Historical Review* (January 1989).

"Social Service by Harvard Students." *Charities* (November 1906).

"A Soldier's Father Urges Bullets for Traitors." *The Literary Digest* (September 15, 1917).

"Supreme Court Rules for Julian Bond." *The Christian Century* (December 21, 1966).

"Supreme Court: Bond's Word." *Newsweek* (December 19, 1966).

"Tennessee." *Collier's, The National Weekly* (July 18, 1925).

"Ten Years for Criticism." *The Literary Digest* (June 15, 1918).

Thomas, Norman. "Conscientious Objector Replies." *The New Republic* (July 7, 1917).

"The Trial of Eugene V. Debs." *The Survey* (September 21, 1918).

"Treason Must Be Made Odious." *The North American Review* 206 (October 1917).

"Trials: Back to Business." *Newsweek* (June 5, 1967).

"Trials: Cuffed." *Newsweek* (June 12, 1967).

"Trials: Nuremberg & Viet Nam." *Time* (May 26, 1967).

"Verbatim Record of Trial of Levy, Howard P., 05 013 082, Captain," on file at the Southern Regional Office of the ACLU (June 1967).

Von Hoffman, Nicholas. "The Conviction of Howard Levy." *The New Republic* (June 17, 1967).

"War's Contradictions—A Pacifist for Conscription." *The Survey* (February 26, 1916).

Williams, David. "They Never Stopped Watching Us." *FBI Political Surveillance* (1924–1936).

Index

About the Author

DIANE GAREY is an Emmy Award®-winning independent film-maker and author based in western Massachusetts. She was editor and, with Lawrence R. Hott, co-producer of the PBS documentary "The ACLU: A History," which won the Gold Apple Award. She has co-produced over a dozen documentaries on subjects ranging from nursing history to the Wilderness Act of 1964, as well as an award-winning feature-length dramatic film about the boyhood of John Muir.